Tuscany

Antipasti Salad

Pan Fried Asparagus

Baked Salmon
with Lemon and Capers

Pizza Margherita

Chocolate Chip Biscotti

Dark Chocolate
Gelato Affogato

Sweet Potato Souffle

Roasted Rainbow Carrots

Meyer Lemon Tart

Spring Time Tea Party

Rooibos Gingersnap Tea

Cucumber and Salmon Bites

Carrots with Olive Tapenade Trio

Orange and Cranberry Scones

Zucchini Bread

SUNDAY

EG
WITH RO
AND BOLETE MU

BRAISED PORK BELLY

SWEET POTATO HASH

CINNAMON MAPLE HOT

Backyard Picnic

Creamy Fennel Slaw
with Carrots and Apples

Balsamic Tomato and Peach Salad

Teriyaki Country Ribs

No'tato Salad

Lemon Blueberry Muffins

Thanksg

Cranberry Relish

Poached Pear

Lemon Green Beans

Apple Veal S

Stuffed Tu
Rubbed with Duck F

Pecan P

...h diced mango

...pper

...h drawn butter

...mango salsa

...mer
...Party

...with Mint

...Shrimp

...cken
...shrooms

...getables

...tice Crust

Easter Lunch

takeout fake-out

first
steamed spring rolls with sesame dipping sauce

soup
wonton soup

main
general tso's chicken

side
stir fried vegetables
shrimp fried cauliower rice
long beans with mushroom sauce

New Yea
Cocktail

Butternut Squa
Shooter

gather

The Art of Paleo Entertaining

Victory Belt Publishing Inc.
Las Vegas

Book design and layout by Bill Staley and Hayley Mason
All photography by Bill Staley and Hayley Mason except:
- Pg 7 (bottom right), 185 photos (top and left) by Heather Lahtinen
- Pg 201 photo by Bobby Gill

Cover Photo Recipes:

Pg 272	Winter Pomegranate Salad with Fig Balsamic Vinaigrette
Pg 274	Candied Yams
Pg 278	Standing Rib Roast

This recipe:

Pg 178	Blackberry Cobbler with Vanilla Bean Ice Cream

for more recipe inspiration, visit www.PrimalPalate.com
also by Hayley and Bill:
Make it Paleo (October, 2011)
The 30 Day Guide to Paleo Cooking (June, 2013)

You don't have to cook fancy or
complicated masterpieces—
just good food from fresh ingredients.

-Julia Child

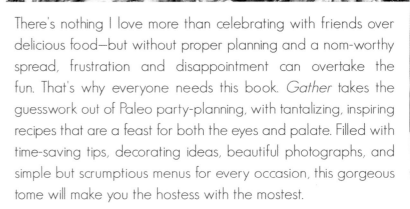

praise for **gather**

In *Gather*, Hayley Mason and Bill Staley have captured the essence of what it means to dine in the finest Primal style. They understand that eating ought to be a visceral pleasure that transcends simply "getting the macronutrient ratios right." They beautifully and artfully cover the entire experience, from the process of selecting and preparing food, to creating a warm and inviting setting and ultimately sharing it with your tribe of friends and loved ones. Of course, their recipes also result in the kinds of delicious meals that turn non-paleos into ardent believers.

—Mark Sisson
author of *The Primal Blueprint* and of MarksDailyApple.com

There's nothing I love more than celebrating with friends over delicious food—but without proper planning and a nom-worthy spread, frustration and disappointment can overtake the fun. That's why everyone needs this book. *Gather* takes the guesswork out of Paleo party-planning, with tantalizing, inspiring recipes that are a feast for both the eyes and palate. Filled with time-saving tips, decorating ideas, beautiful photographs, and simple but scrumptious menus for every occasion, this gorgeous tome will make you the hostess with the mostest.

—Michelle Tam
award winning blogger at NomNomPaleo.com

Holidays and gatherings are a time to celebrate—and food is often the centerpiece of the event! In *Gather*, Hayley Mason and Bill Staley show us how eating a healthy, grain-free diet can include many of your old favorites while introducing your friends and loved ones to fantastic new dishes. This stunning book walks us through creating delicious menus for any occasion—filled with fresh flavors and amazing recreations of old favorites that will certainly wow your guests.

—Diane Sanfilippo
author of the *New York Times* Bestselling book, *Practical Paleo*

If you're on a Paleo diet and you love food, this book is for you. A lot of early Paleo cookbooks were long on health but short on flavor and creativity. Bill & Hayley's book is proof that it's possible to eat and entertain like a gourmet without gluten, grains or other "non-Paleo" ingredients. If you're a Paleo foodie like I am, *Gather* is a must on your kitchen shelf.

—Chris Kresser, M.S. L.Ac
among the "top 50 most influential people in health and fitness"

In *Gather*, Hayley Mason and Bill Staley serve up a feast for the eyes, the spirit and the stomach. The authors have crafted a foolproof recipe for hosting successful special events. From the detailed organization tips, to the beautifully themed décor suggestions and finally the perfectly complementing flavors and creative menus, your friends and family will clamor for invitations to these simply designed, healthy soirées!

—Mira Calton, CN and Jayson Calton, PhD
authors of *Naked Calories* and *Rich Food, Poor Food*

Hayley Mason and Bill Staley are true masters of the art of delicious, beautiful, nourishing food, yet their greatest talent is something even more powerful than that. Hayley and Bill have the gift of translating their elegant taste into something both instinctual and accessible. With *Gather*, they have awakened that primal desire within us all to share the gift of food, and they've done so while harnessing the deeply-rooted sense of joy and creativity that lies within each of us.

—Liz Wolfe, NTP
author of *Modern Cave Girl*

Every day is a new opportunity to make better decisions involving our food. Sometimes our excitement is so grand that this admirable pursuance opens the floodgates for frustration, doubts, and eventually failure. What we require is a beautifully designed, structured approach to tackle the most daunting situations. Case and point, you have the responsibility of cooking Christmas dinner for six while catering to various food allergies. Fret not, the beautiful minds of Hayley Mason and Bill Staley have composed a stunning masterpiece of carefully planned gatherings designed to transform you into the Gordon Ramsey of the Paleo world with a touch of class rivaling the Queen of England.

—George Bryant
author of *Caveman Feast* and CivilizedCavemanCooking.com

Martha Stewart meets Cro Magnon! Bill Staley and Hayley Mason have taken the Paleo experience out of the sweat of Crossfit gyms, away from the forest and savannah, and launched an elegant 21st century interpretation of this lifestyle. No preceding Paleo cookbook has cast these ideas into such a luxurious and cultured setting, all viewed from the perspective of gathering and entertaining. Beautifully photographed, with uniquely clever approaches to the menu, such as Night in Tuscany, Takeout Fake-out, and Hunter-Gatherer Feast, *Gather* will be a classic favorite for grain-free living.

—Dr. William Davis
#1 *New York Times* Bestselling author of *Wheat Belly*

a note from Hayley and Bill

What you hold in your hands is a Paleo *lifestyle* cookbook, not a Paleo *diet* cookbook. In the last few years, we've noticed several ways people find the Paleo diet. Whether they find it through a CrossFit gym, in an attempt to manage a chronic disease, or as a means of weight loss and health improvement, the Paleo diet ultimately becomes a lifestyle after a short period as a "diet." A lifestyle, unlike a diet, includes allowances for holidays, special occasions, and celebrations. We believe following a Paleo lifestyle is the best way to nourish our bodies, so we wrote this book to help people maintain a healthy lifestyle while also enjoying their lives!

Throughout the process of writing this book, we had many wonderful opportunities to entertain large groups of our family members and friends. It was clear to us, week after week, that serving good, "Paleo-friendly" food did not need an excuse or an explanation. When you serve dishes made with real, fresh ingredients, they speak for themselves. The meals also sparked lively conversations about the benefits of eating a grain-free diet. Food has an amazing way of bringing people together, and when you do so with healthy food, it has the power to drive dramatic change. It is our hope that this book will do the same for you. By bringing you and your friends together, it will hopefully influence more people to start eating real food.

We are both foodies at heart. We love artistic food styling, gourmet ingredients, and celebrating with friends and family.

Our personal everyday diets are full of nutrient-dense foods that are low in sugar, but when it comes to celebrations, we feel it's important to pay tribute to family traditions. In writing *Gather*, we wanted to create a cookbook with recipes to fit a relaxed Paleo lifestyle, focusing on celebrations with loved ones. We have included recipes to encourage a healthy relationship with your food that won't leave you feeling as if you're missing out on life's special moments.

Menus for birthdays, holidays, everyday family gatherings, and a multitude of other special occasions are all covered in this book. You won't find macronutrient breakdowns with the recipes, and most menus contain a dessert. We believe it's better to eat grain-free treats than to go completely "off the wagon" with conventional, gluten-laden sweets. As it is in our daily lives, our approach to cooking in this book is laid back and sustainable.

So, we hope that *Gather* will inspire you to cook for friends. The meals don't have to be elaborate, exotic, or even complicated. We have found more than anything that people respond to the magic of real ingredients, seasoned simply and cooked well. We feel that the best gatherings are those with close family and friends who cook together from start to finish. Our favorite memories involve several family members cooking together, laughing together, and enjoying it all together.

a year of
gatherings

spring

18   Takeout Fake-out
    24   "Wonton" Soup
    26   Steamed Spring Rolls with Sesame
            Dipping Sauce
    28   Stir-Fried Vegetables
    30   Shrimp Fried Cauliflower Rice
    32   Long Beans with Mushroom Sauce
    34   General Tso's Chicken
    36   Almond Cookies

38   Casual Sunday Brunch
    44   Eggs Benedict with Roasted Asparagus
            and Bolete Mushrooms
    46   Braised Pork Belly
    48   Sweet Potato Hash with Rosemary
    50   Cinnamon Maple Hot Cakes

52   Springtime Tea Party
    58   Rooibos Gingersnap Tea
    60   Cucumber and Salmon Bites
    60   Carrots with Olive Tapenade Trio
    62   Orange Scones and Cranberry Scones
    64   Zucchini Bread

66   Easter Lunch
    72   Avocado Cream Eggs
    74   Grapefruit Salad
    76   Honey Glazed Ham
    78   Sweet Potato Soufflé
    80   Roasted Rainbow Carrots
    82   Meyer Lemon Tart

84   Backyard Picnic
    90   Teriyaki Country Ribs
    92   No'tato Salad
    94   Creamy Fennel Slaw with Carrots and Apples
    96   Balsamic Tomato and Peach Salad
    98   Lemon Blueberry Muffins

summer

100   A Night in Tuscany
    106   Antipasti Salad
    108   Pan-Fried Asparagus
    110   Baked Salmon with Lemon and Capers
    112   Pizza Margherita
    114   Chocolate Chip Biscotti
    116   Affogato with Dark Chocolate Gelato

118   Midsummer Garden Party
    124   Watermelon Salad with Mint
    124   Bacon-Wrapped Shrimp
    126   Pan-Seared Chicken with Onions
            and Mushrooms
    128   Grilled Balsamic Vegetables
    130   Green Bean Salad with Artichoke Hearts and Olives
    132   Apple Pie with a Lattice Crust

134   Tropical Getaway
    140   Micro-Greens Salad with Diced Mango
    142   Stuffed Red Snapper
    144   Spiny Lobster Tails with Drawn Butter
    146   Fried Plantains with Mango Salsa

148 A Taste of Cuba
    154   Yuca con Mojo (Yuca with Garlic Sauce)
    156   Costillitas (Cuban Baby Back Ribs)
    158   Pescados Asado (Grilled Fish)
    160   Arroz Azafrán (Saffron Rice)
    162   Flan de Coco (Coconut Flan)

164 Urban Escape
    170   Crab-Stuffed Artichoke Bottoms
    172   Spiced Nuts with Rosemary and Thyme
    174   Pan-Seared Lamb Chops with Rhubarb Chutney
    176   Sautéed Japanese Eggplant and Onions with Sage
    178   Blackberry Cobbler with Vanilla Bean Ice Cream

fall

180 Harvest Dinner
    186   Cherry and Walnut Salad with Fig Balsamic Vinaigrette
    188   Pumpkin Chicken Chili
    190   Apple-Glazed Pork Loin
    192   Honeycrisp Applesauce
    194   Baked Acorn Squash
    196   Pumpkin Torte with Cream Cheese Frosting and Caramel

198 Spooky Supper
    204   Roasted Marrow Bones
    204   Ghostly Pear Guacamole with Fried Plantain Chips
    206   Beef Heart Stew
    208   Spaghetti and "Eyeballs"
    210   "Bleeding" Cupcakes
    212   Mummy Cookies Black and White Bones
    214   Caramel Crab Apples

216 Thanksgiving Feast
    222   Cranberry Relish
    224   Poached Pear Salad
    226   Lemon Green Beans with Shallots
    228   Apple Veal Stuffing
    230   Stuffed Turkey Rubbed with Duck Fat and Herbs
    232   Pecan Pie

winter

234 Hunter-Gatherer Feast
    240   Sweet and Tangy Venison Meatballs
    242   Wild Mushroom Soup
    244   Apple-Scented Venison Roast
    246   Grilled Elk Chops with Port Wine Reduction
    248   Petite Potato Trio
    250   Crème Brûlée

252 Birthday Celebration
    258   Spinach and Artichoke Dip with Herb Crackers
    260   Pork Sliders and Veggie Sliders
    262   Chicken Nuggets with Honey Mustard
    264   Checkerboard Cake

266 Winter Holiday
    272   Winter Pomegranate Salad with Fig Balsamic Vinaigrette
    274   Candied Yams
    276   Standing Rib Roast with Horseradish Sauce
    278   Roasted Green and Purple Cabbage
    280   Yorkshire Puddings
    282   Sour Cream Coffee Cake

284 New Year's Cocktail Party
    290   Butternut Squash Soup Shooters
    292   Pigs in a Blanket
    294   Crostini with Goat Cheese and Fig Compote
    296   Antipasti Skewers
    298   Mini Chocolate Martinis

planning a gathering

The word "entertaining" is one that has the ability to strike fear in the minds of cooks everywhere. What's more, entertaining for a crowd of Paleo folks seems downright impossible, right? Wrong! Sure, there is a bit of an art to orchestrating an elegant Paleo gathering, but with a little bit of planning and organization, it can be a fun and simple affair.

In this book, we show you how to design the perfect Paleo meal to enjoy with family and friends, from the big ideas right down to the tiniest of details. If you take nothing else away from our overview, know this: Entertaining is meant to be fun for the guests and the host. If the host is not having a good time, there's a strong chance the guests won't either. So, sit back, take a deep breath, and relax because this is going to be a lot of fun.

Why entertain?

The first stop in this odyssey of planning knowledge is the "why" and "how" of creating a special meal for Paleo guests. Simply put, the Paleo diet (though we refer to it as a lifestyle from here on in) is a way of eating that essentially emphasizes the consumption of plants and animals. That doesn't sound so bad, right? Meals generally consist of a main course that has protein at its core, a few side dishes that are vegetable-centric, and possibly some appetizers or desserts that recreate some grain-free favorites. The recipes in this book are geared toward special occasions, as you'll see in the following pages, and with special occasions comes a little special splurging. For more information on the dietary suggestions that support the Paleo lifestyle, visit our website, The Food Lovers Kitchen (www.PrimalPalate.com).

The basic elements of planning

For the gathering you are planning, it may turn out that you have a mixed group of people; some that follow the Paleo lifestyle, and others that do not. Have no fear—the recipes in this cookbook were created to fill the common ground between the two and satisfy everyone's palates for good food. The important thing is to read and find the ingredients ahead of time. If you're new to the Paleo lifestyle, don't purchase any food containing gluten—ever. This is rule "numero uno," and a non-negotiable point in our minds. To put it another way, serving a recipe with gluten hidden in it would be like offering a vegetable dish cooked in beef broth to a vegan. Check the ingredients of any canned or prepackaged foods, and avoid grains, soy, food colorings, food preservatives, chemicals, and polyunsaturated fats such as canola oil, peanut oil, soybean oil, safflower oil, sunflower oil, and grapeseed oil.

It's fun for us to take our old favorite meals and make them Paleo. That was actually the premise of our first book *Make it Paleo* (clever, right?) and an underlying theme we continue to use in our cooking. Recreating popular recipes into Paleo meals is a great way to show people just how manageable the Paleo lifestyle can be. With recipes like General Tso's Chicken (pg 34), Pizza Margherita (pg 112), and even a Checkerboard Cake (pg 264), it will be easy to show anyone a realistic version of the Paleo lifestyle.

The first step in planning any type of gathering is to identify the occasion you intend to celebrate. Is it a holiday? A birthday? A bridal or baby shower? It could even be just getting a few old friends together for a weeknight supper. The next step is to consider what type of theme you would like the gathering to follow. That's where this book comes in handy with 17 themes and menus to get your creativity flowing. Selecting a theme for your party will influence the menu, table decorations, and other party elements, so give the theme careful thought.

Inviting people to your gathering

After you know the occasion and theme of the gathering, select a time for the party, and draft a guest list. When selecting a date, give some thought to when people will be free to attend. Usually, weekend nights are best. Also be sure to give yourself plenty of preparation time and clean up time before and after the gathering.

In today's world of Facebook events and Evites, sending a written invitation may seem like a thing of the past, if not a waste of time. But a traditional invitation is a great way to show that you have taken a lot of care in planning your event. Send invitations at least two weeks in advance for casual gatherings, giving up to one month for more formal occasions like holidays and birthday parties. Personalizing your invitation for the theme of your gathering is a fun way to get your guests excited. Always include a small RSVP card, along with an envelope and postage so that your guests can effortlessly respond to your invitation. They will really appreciate that you took the extra time.

Depending upon the occasion, it may be simple to select guests. A private holiday dinner, for example, may be exclusively for family members. If you're thinking of hosting a dinner with a mixed list of guests, consider their interests and personalities, and how they might fit together. Seat those guests with common interests near one another to make conversation natural. On the opposite end of the spectrum, if you're inviting a few guests you know don't get along, be sure to sit them on opposite ends of the dinner table. While the idea of assigned seating may seem formal or old fashioned, it's usually a good idea to have a plan about where to seat key people at the table. Guests are often thrilled to see their name in front of their plate. Little details like this go a long way toward making the night special.

Developing a great menu

Once you have taken care of the occasion, theme, guest list, and invites, the next step is to lay out the menu for the event. To start, consider the seasonal produce that may be available. We enjoy shopping at farmers markets during the warmer months, and we also make it a point to stay in touch with local farmers throughout the winter months to get the best meats possible. Cooking for your guests with the freshest foods will bring the best flavors to the table for your meal.

Also consider the degree of formality of your event. For casual events, family-style serving or buffet-style may be appropriate. For more formal events, restaurant-style plating of each dish may be best. This will influence the types of dishes you choose. Also consider how many people are coming, and how much time you will have to cook and prepare before the party. Do not overextend your capabilities. If you only have three hours to prepare on a Friday evening after work, do yourself a favor and avoid trying to create a nine-course tasting menu! Similarly, if you're hosting a formal dinner for twenty, a buffet with a large salad, entrée, and single side dish may be underwhelming. Whatever the case may be, be sure to match the number or courses and degree of difficulty to the occasion.

Your table doesn't have to be covered in Pottery Barn attire to impress guests. Thrift stores, flea markets, craft stores, and party stores are great places to find interesting, affordable gems for decorating your table. Some of our favorite table settings were a mix of old and new, including items we found at local antique shops.

Timing is everything

Timing everything just right is vital when planning your event. There's the timing of the party itself when choosing a date and time of day. There's the timing of shopping and cooking of certain dishes prior to the party. There's the timing of guests arriving (be specific on that one so as to avoid confusion).

The menu should also follow the theme of the party. This book contains a wealth of menu inspiration, and beyond its pages you can find even more menu ideas on our website, www.PrimalPalate.com.

A few days before the meal, start shopping for ingredients and decorations. At this point, you can buy ingredients that will last or items for dishes that will be prepared ahead of time. It may be necessary to make a second trip to the store if you're cooking highly perishable items like fresh fish. As with the other elements of thinking through your gathering, a bit of strategic planning is key. Make the most of your preparation time, including one or two consolidated trips to buy ingredients and decorations.

With the theme as your guide, start looking for simple effects that will help reinforce the aesthetic you have in mind. If you truly need to buy new things, strive to find elements that can be reused year to year or that will blend in with your other decor. Colored napkins and interesting napkin rings can go a long way. Add a centerpiece of fresh flowers, and that may be all you need to set a beautiful table.

Then, during the party, timing elements get even more critical as dishes need to be served. The cadence of the party should flow smoothly for the guests. As they arrive, offer to take their coats, or make some other gesture to help them feel as comfortable as possible. Generally, this is also a good time to take a drink order or show them to the bar area if you've gone that route. It helps to have some degree of flexibility on the front end of the party since some guests could arrive late.

If alcohol is being consumed during dinner, it should be available at all times prior to the food being served. The better host will have ample food and drinks on hand for guests, often more than the situation seems to require (just in case).

It's up to you as the host to indicate when it's time to take a seat at the table or start getting food from a buffet. You will control the pace of the party, so be sure to pay attention to guests as you're making final cooking preparations. For appetizers and cocktails, thirty to forty-five minutes prior to the dinner is usually enough, although up to sixty minutes is more appropriate for some crowds. The first course should be served promptly upon seating and conclude within fifteen minutes. The timing of subsequent courses can vary, as the pace of dinner is relative to the type of occasion you're celebrating. As the meal winds down, it may be appropriate to offer your guests a cup of coffee or some other kind of drink. This can serve as a subtle cue that the evening is drawing to a close.

Details make it memorable

The details of your event will be what make it memorable. These details include the place settings at the table, the decorations, linens, and other serving items. If you're just starting to build your collection of serving ware, don't worry because building an elegant collection from scratch is easy. The most common route people take is selecting neutral colored plates or even just white. We have an enormous collection of white plates, white serving platters of all shapes and sizes, and other white table elements. It's immensely helpful to have a variety of serving ware options on hand, but even just a few select pieces are a great start.

We would be lost without a big white platter, however. It seems like there is always a dish that requires a large platter, so it gets plenty of use. We also have a medium-sized rectangular platter, which works well for side dishes and appetizers. A large shallow bowl will work well for serving family-style salads and can also hold a generously portioned side dish. Finally, we have a few Le Creuset enameled baking dishes that are classy enough to bring right to the table in any situation. The bright colors and classic styling are easy to incorporate into nearly any theme, and you'll see us do just that throughout this book.

For glassware, we also prefer simple pieces as our mainstays and sometimes incorporate a few fancier types for embellishment. We have a relatively plain, yet nice set of Crate & Barrel glasses that are classy enough for a formal dinner, yet can also make a casual weeknight dinner feel special. It's hard to go the opposite direction, trying to make less formal glassware work in a more formal setting, so we recommend going with slightly higher end glasses. That's not to say that everyday glasses don't have their place, but when entertaining, it's usually occasion enough to bring out the good stuff.

Our theory on silverware follows suit with the theme of keeping staple items a bit neutral. The table decorations, centerpieces, and linens play more of a role in dressing up the occasion anyway. Silverware should feel sturdy and be clean of water spots. Take a few moments in advance of the event to inspect your silverware, and polish it if necessary. If the event is on the formal side, use the opportunity to bring out your good silver. Of course, sterling and silver-plated utensils will likely require polishing before the meal, so be sure to allocate some time for that.

Linens, which include napkins, table runners, and tablecloths, are a central part of the table decor. Be creative, and don't get too "matchy-matchy." Mixing solids and patterns is fun. We have a few patterned table runners that we accent with colored napkins that match one of the colors in the runner. We even have a set of colored napkins that are each different in their own right, making for colorful and creative table settings! We love the simple elegance of just using a table runner instead of a tablecloth. While some situations call for the full coverage of a tablecloth, we prefer runners because they can add a splash of color down the center of the table. If you have a beautiful table that you love, it's great to show it off and not hide it under a cloth. It's often easier to clean a spill on a bare table than a tablecloth.

And while we're on the topic of spills, accidents do happen. So, as a host, don't get upset when someone tips a glass of wine or drops a pork chop. It's bound to happen, and a spot treatment on a linen isn't worth making your guest feel guilty.

Pulling it all together

The final element for decorating the table is the centerpiece. Our favorite choice for table decoration is fresh cut flowers, though we like to change our styles with the seasons. Floral centerpieces are

classic and almost always appropriate. Keep arrangements low, however, so that people can talk across the table during dinner. If your arrangement has the potential to obstruct conversation, simply remove it from the dinner table while people are eating.

We often choose to have several smaller decorations that can remain on the table at all times, regardless of the centerpiece. In the fall, we like to set out small pumpkins, Indian corn, small gourds, and acorns. Wintertime is all about citrus, evergreen boughs, and pinecones. Spring and summer bring flowers that are hard to resist, though fresh berries or other interesting produce is another great way to spice up your table during these seasons. Who doesn't love a decoration they can snack on? Sometimes, inspiration will strike at odd times for decorations. A few days before our "Night in Tuscany" dinner shoot, small ornate olive trees suddenly appeared in our local Whole Foods. While relying on luck is a flimsy strategy, thinking outside the box can yield some nice results.

In the course of working on this book, the two of us got even better at entertaining than when we started. Of course, it was entertaining with the addition of recipe development and photo shoots, which is a bit more intense than your average dinner party. While we learned quite a bit about being good hosts, we gained incredible insight into the less tangible aspects of hosting. A good host will make guests feel completely at ease, even if things are going haywire in the kitchen.

Entertaining is less about putting on a flawless gourmet dinner than it is about pulling family and friends together for a good time. The true art of entertaining is finding the delicate balance between playing a good host, cooking a fabulous meal, and enjoying the party yourself. Only with practice will this balance become intuitive for many hosts, which is all the more reason to entertain more often!

takeout fake-out

Chinese food, or an Americanized version of it, seems to be available on every street corner and in every mall food court across America. While authentic Chinese food is generally based on fresh ingredients, most fast food versions are full of crap and chemicals.

When I (Bill) was growing up, my dad (Bill Sr.) spent a lot of time in China and Japan for work. He loved the cuisine and culture of the Far East, and when he was home, my mother did her best to recreate the foods he enjoyed while away on business. For nearly 30 years, my mother has regularly cooked Chinese dishes for our family. We were lucky because our reference point for "takeout" was homemade and full of fresh ingredients.

Now, as a young soon-to-be-married couple, we make Chinese dishes all the time. If we're in a hurry, we can throw together a stir-fry in almost no time. On those rare occasions when we have the time to really focus on cooking, we make some of the dishes in this menu.

Mastering a grain-free General Tso's Chicken was quite an accomplishment for us. I've had that dish more times than I can count, and I can say with confidence that it's one of my favorites. We're certain you'll find our version to be every bit as good as the restaurant one, just without the bad ingredients.

To make this meal feel as authentic as possible, we did a bit of shopping at our local Asian foods market. If yours is anything like the one in our town, you'll find incredible deals on everything from obscure, exotic ingredients to authentic serving ware. Even if it's a bit out of the way, these stores are often quite impressive in terms of the breadth of produce they carry.

This menu contains a variety of popular Chinese dishes, all so good that you'll be able to convince almost anyone that it's takeout!

menu

. . . .

"Wonton" Soup

Steamed Spring Rolls
with Sesame Dipping Sauce

Stir-Fried Vegetables

Shrimp Fried Cauliflower Rice

Long Beans with Mushroom Sauce

General Tso's Chicken

Almond Cookies

Shopping and Preparation

Our Chinese menu was a challenging one to style. We decided to shop around our local Asian food market and were pleasantly surprised to find lots of fun authentic plates for this menu. We also popped into a local Chinese restaurant and purchased a few takeout containers to send leftovers home with guests.

Since your table will be filled with beautiful Chinese food, as well as colorful authentic plates and serving dishes, a simple orchid plant is a great way to add elegance to the centerpiece. The food will style your table for you, so keep the settings simple.

Three days ahead

Search for fun, authentic plates, serving platters, chopsticks, and spoons. Visit your local Chinese food restaurant and grab some takeout containers to really wow your guests when it's time to pack up the leftovers.

One day ahead

Finish your shopping for fresh produce, flowers, and any items you may have forgotten. You can also make the almond cookies, the "wonton" soup, and the filling for the spring rolls. You can set your table today as well, so that it's all ready for tomorrow.

One hour before dinner

As your guests arrive, pour drinks, and start plating dishes. Your guests will be impressed as you bring out all of the beautiful food.

"wonton" soup

This soup doesn't look like the wonton soup you usually see in Chinese restaurants. That's because we've ditched the wonton wrappers! Don't worry; all of the familiar flavors of this popular soup are still there, and we're sure you'll enjoy it just as much!

Meatballs

1 pound pork

6-8 large shrimp, minced

1/8 cup green onion, chopped

Salt and pepper to taste

1 tablespoon garlic, minced

1 tablespoon ginger, minced

2 drops fish sauce

2 tablespoons coconut aminos

2 tablespoons duck fat

Broth

2 quarts chicken stock

2 tablespoons coconut aminos

3 drops fish sauce

Salt and pepper to taste

1/4 cup green onions

Preheat your oven to 350 degrees. To prepare the meatballs, combine the pork, minced shrimp, green onion, salt, pepper, garlic, ginger, fish sauce, and 1 tablespoon of the coconut aminos in a large mixing bowl.

Form the mixture into small 3/4-inch balls, and place them on a parchment-lined baking sheet. Bake the meatballs for 15 minutes.

In a large skillet, heat the duck fat over medium heat. Fry the meatballs in the duck fat until they are brown on all sides. Splash the meatballs with additional (about 1 tablespoon) coconut aminos. Once the meatballs are brown, remove them from the heat.

For the broth, in a large saucepan, bring the chicken stock to a boil. Add the coconut aminos, fish sauce, salt, and pepper. Stir to combine, and continue to boil.

Add the meatballs to the broth, along with the green onions, and stir. Boil the meatballs for 5 minutes, reduce the heat to low, and cover.

Simmer for at least one hour or until you are ready to serve (whichever comes first).

Serves 8

steamed spring rolls with sesame dipping sauce

Steamed cabbage leaves are a great way to enjoy the flavors of Chinese spring rolls. Cabbage offers more security then a lettuce wrap, so your fillings will be sure to stay put!

In a steamer pot, steam the cabbage leaves until they can fold easily (about 5-10 minutes). While the cabbage leaves are steaming, heat 2 tablespoons of duck fat in a heavy skillet. Sauté the diced pork for 4-5 minutes, adding the coconut aminos to season the pork. Add the carrots, celery, and mushrooms to the skillet and sauté for an additional 3 minutes. Remove the skillet from the heat and reserve the filling until the cabbage leaves are ready to roll.

Trim each steamed cabbage leaf to create uniform shapes, cutting large leaves in half. Place a small amount of the filling in the center of each cabbage leaf. To roll wraps, fold in the side closest to you, and roll slightly. Fold the ends toward the center, and roll to seal. Place into a steamer basket, seal side down, and steam for 10 minutes.

For the dipping sauce, you will need a small saucepan. Add the coconut aminos to the pan, along with the toasted sesame oil, garlic, ginger root, salt, and pepper. Warm over medium heat while whisking until the garlic and ginger are soft and have infused the sauce.

Serve in several small dishes, spread around the table so that your guests have easy access to the sauce.

Serves 8

Spring Rolls
12-15 cabbage leaves
2 tablespoons duck fat
1/2 pound pork, diced
2 tsp coconut aminos
3 carrots, julienned
3 celery stalks, julienned
1/2 cup mushrooms, sliced

Dipping Sauce
1/4 cup coconut aminos
1/8 cup toasted sesame oil
1 clove garlic, minced
1/2 teaspoon ginger root, minced
Salt and pepper to taste

2 tablespoons duck fat

3 cups broccoli, cut into bite-sized pieces

2 cups bok choy, stems removed

1 tablespoon toasted sesame oil

3 tablespoons coconut oil

3 drops fish sauce

1 cup carrot, sliced

1/2 cup celery

1 cup snow peas

Salt and pepper to taste

1/2 cup bamboo shoots

1/2 cup water chestnuts

1 tablespoon toasted sesame seeds

stir-fried vegetables

With a little bit of everything, stir-fried vegetables epitomize the meaning of a quick, "throw-it-together" dish. This is something you can make on the fly and feed an army in the process. The water chestnuts and bamboo shoots add unusual textures to the dish, while the flavor of the sesame oil provides nice dimension.

In a large wok or skillet, bring two tablespoons of duck fat to frying temperature (300 degrees) over medium-high heat. Carefully place the broccoli and bok choy in the skillet, and stir until they are slightly soft.

Add the toasted sesame oil, coconut oil, and fish sauce. Once mixed, toss in the carrot, celery, and snow peas, and continue to sauté. Sprinkle with salt and pepper.

Finally, add the bamboo shoots and water chestnuts, and stir-fry until all ingredients are cooked. Sprinkle with the toasted sesame seeds to garnish.

Serves 8

shrimp fried cauliflower rice

No takeout Chinese meal would be complete without a side order of rice. But what do you do if you're not eating rice or any grains at all? Simple—you make cauliflower rice! This dish has all of the amazing flavors of traditional fried rice without the guilt.

In a large wok or skillet, heat the duck fat over medium heat. Add the shallots, red and green bell peppers, and carrot to the skillet, and sauté for 3-4 minutes.

Add the shrimp to the skillet, continuing to sauté. Once the shrimp is pink on all sides, add the coconut aminos, fish sauce, and toasted sesame oil. When the shrimp is cooked thoroughly, add the whisked egg and sauté until the egg is scrambled and cooked through.

Rinse the cauliflower, and cut into large chunks. "Rice" the cauliflower using the coarse side of a box grater, or with a food processor using a shredding disc. Add the riced cauliflower and green onion. Sprinkle with salt and pepper to taste, and sauté lightly until the cauliflower is tender.

Serves 8

1 tablespoon duck fat

1/4 cup shallots, diced

1/2 cup red bell peppers, diced

1/2 cup green bell peppers, diced

1 large carrot, peeled and diced

2 cups shrimp, peeled and de-veined

3 tablespoons coconut aminos

3 drops fish sauce

1/2 tablespoon toasted sesame oil

1 egg, whisked

4 cups riced cauliflower

1/4 green onion

Salt and pepper to taste

long beans with mushroom sauce

Chinese long beans are commonly used in the cuisine of Southeast Asia. Though usually in stir-fry recipes, they are steamed in this dish until they're tender. Then, they're dressed with a thick and creamy mushroom sauce. You'll never want them any other way!

In a large pot, steam the long beans until fork tender (about 20 minutes).

Meanwhile, in a small saucepan, heat the duck fat over medium heat, and add the oyster mushrooms to the pan. Sauté them, and add the coconut aminos, chicken stock, and fish sauce. Briskly whisk in the arrowroot flour. Increase the heat, and whisk the mixture until the arrowroot dissolves and thickens. Add salt and pepper to taste.

Plate the long beans, and pour the mushroom sauce over the beans to coat.

Serves 8

2 pounds long beans
1 teaspoon duck fat
1/2 cup oyster mushrooms, diced
2 tablespoons coconut aminos
1/3 cup chicken stock
2 drops fish sauce
1 teaspoon arrowroot flour
Salt and pepper to taste

general tso's chicken

You might be surprised to learn that this dish is not a traditional Chinese dish, but rather one created by Chinese restaurants in America. General Tso's chicken is widely enjoyed, and some would say coveted by those who enjoy Chinese food (or at least the American version of it). We would happily pit this Paleo version of the dish against any conventional version on the grounds of taste, texture, and general deliciousness. Be sure to give yourself ample time to make the dish, as it can take up to an hour.

3 pounds boneless, skinless chicken thighs

1 cup duck fat

1/8 cup green onion, thinly sliced

Batter

1 egg

1/4 cup coconut aminos

1 cup arrowroot flour

Sauce

16 ounces chicken broth

1/2 cup maple syrup (or 1/2 teaspoon liquid Stevia extract)

1/2 cup coconut aminos

1/4 cup white vinegar

1/2 cup arrowroot flour

2 teaspoons duck fat

1 1/2 teaspoons fresh garlic, minced

1 teaspoon salt

1 1/2 cups green onions, sliced

3 small dried chilies

Rinse the chicken under cool water, and pat it dry. Cut the chicken into 1-inch cubes, and set it aside.

In a medium-sized mixing bowl, whisk together the egg and coconut aminos. Add in the arrowroot flour until the mixture is thick and evenly combined. Toss this mixture with the cubed chicken until the chicken is evenly coated.

In a medium sized mixing bowl, whisk together the chicken broth, maple syrup, coconut aminos, white vinegar and arrowroot flour. Whisk until the arrowroot is completely dissolved. In a large sauce pan, heat the duck fat over medium heat and add the minced garlic. Saute the minced garlic for 30 seconds, then pour in the broth. Season with salt and bring the sauce to a boil while whisking. Once the sauce has thickened, reduce the heat and stir in the green onions and dried chilies. Simmer on low heat until serving.

In a large Dutch oven over medium-high heat, heat the duck fat. Test the heat with a single piece of chicken. It should sizzle when the oil is up to temperature. Place the chicken in half of the Dutch oven, and allow it to cook on one side for 3-4 minutes. Flip, and place more chicken in the other half of the Dutch oven. By working this way, you keep the temperature of the oil hot and consistent. Adding too much chicken at once cools it down.

Remove the chicken from the Dutch oven after frying. Add the sauce to the remaining duck fat in the Dutch oven, and bring it to a boil. Add in the chicken, toss quickly to coat, and remove it from heat.

Garnish with the remaining 1/8 cup of green onion, and serve.

Serves 8

almond cookies

Chinese almond cookies are traditionally served along with green or Oolong tea as a symbol of good luck during Chinese New Year celebrations. These cookies have a delightfully fluffy, yet slightly chewy, texture. Serve them warm with orange slices at the end of dinner.

2 cups blanched almond flour

1/2 teaspoon salt

1 1/2 teaspoons gluten-free baking powder

1/4 cup arrowroot flour

1 teaspoon pure vanilla extract

2 teaspoons almond extract

1/2 cup maple syrup

1/2 cup grass-fed butter, melted

24 raw almonds

Preheat your oven to 325 degrees. In a medium-sized mixing bowl, combine the blanched almond flour, salt, baking powder, and arrowroot flour.

In a separate small mixing bowl, combine the vanilla extract, almond extract, maple syrup, and melted butter. Blend with a hand mixer until smooth.

Add the dry ingredients to the wet ingredients, and blend with a hand mixer until the batter is smooth.

Place 1 tablespoon-sized amounts of batter onto a parchment lined baking sheet. Bake for 5 minutes, remove from the oven, and place a raw almond in the center of each cookie. Return the baking sheet to the oven, and bake for an additional 15 minutes. Allow the cookies to cool before serving.

Serves 8

casual sunday brunch

Around the middle of summer, we found out that Hayley's aunt and uncle, Justine and Tony, would be moving out of their home of ten years into a beautiful new house. Over the years, their home had been the place for entertaining in our family. We were both witness to many parties, as they graciously welcomed family and friends time and time again. Justine and Tony are the epitome of entertaining grace and success.

When we found out that they would be moving, it saddened both of us. Our fond memories of many enjoyable meals there would soon come to an end. So, without hesitation, we planned a send-off brunch at their home as a last family meal before the big move. Although we didn't have the whole family there, it was nice knowing that the last gathering in their home would be sealed away forever in this book.

We designed the menu to be simple and diverse. After all, when making brunch, you only have a little time to prepare dishes. Eggs Benedict is the true star of the show and should be prepared last in an effort to serve it hot. The braised pork belly and sweet potato hash can be made first, and then set to cook while you prepare other dishes. Brunch should be all about keeping stress levels low, with simple yet elegant dishes.

menu

· ·

Eggs Benedict with Roasted Asparagus and
Bolete Mushrooms

Braised Pork Belly

Sweet Potato Hash with Rosemary

Cinnamon Maple Hot Cakes

Shopping and Preparation

Five days ahead

Prepare for table settings, and decide on a color theme. Look for wild growing flowers in your yard or at your local market for the centerpiece.

At this point, you can gather almost all of your needed groceries for the meal—eggs, ham, butter, sweet potatoes, onions, carrots, chicken stock, dried bolete mushrooms, champagne, and orange juice (for mimosas, of course). Be sure you also have all of the dry ingredients on hand for the pancakes—coconut flour, baking soda, ground cinnamon, and maple sugar.

One day ahead

Purchase fresh fruit, asparagus, pork belly, and fresh flowers.

The night before the brunch

Braise the pork belly and vegetables. Allow the pork belly to cool, and refrigerate it until the next morning. You can also prep the sweet potato hash the night before, refrigerate it, and heat it again the next morning. An alternative is to prep the hash and keep it sealed in a bag until the next morning. Wash the fruit, arrange it on a platter, cover, and refrigerate overnight.

Three hours before brunch

Set the table, and set out all serving platters that you will need for the meal.

One hour before brunch

Allow the pork belly and sweet potato hash to come to room temperature, and prep other food items for cooking.

Thirty minutes before guests arrive

Place the asparagus dish in the oven to roast, and make the Hollandaise sauce.

As your guests arrive

As guests arrive, pour the mimosas, and set out the fresh fruit platter. Place the pork belly and sweet potato hash in the oven to warm while the asparagus finishes roasting, and fry up the pancakes. Plate the hash and pancakes, and set them on the table along with the pork belly, extra butter, salt and pepper shakers, filtered or sparkling water, and maple syrup.

Plate the asparagus dish in preparation for the poached eggs. Poach the eggs until desired doneness, and place them over the top of the ham slices, asparagus, and mushrooms. Top with a drizzle of Hollandaise sauce, and garnish with slices of green onion. Bring fresh fruit to the dining table so that your guests can enjoy fruit with brunch if they desire, and serve the eggs Benedict.

Hollandaise Sauce
  4 egg yolks
  1 tablespoon freshly squeezed lemon juice
  1/2 teaspoon salt
  Pinch cayenne pepper
  10 tablespoons grass-fed butter,
    melted over low heat

Roasted Asparagus with Bolete Mushrooms
  2 pounds asparagus
  1 tablespoon coconut oil, melted
  1 loosely packed cup dried
    bolete mushrooms, chopped
  Salt and pepper to taste

Eggs Benedict
  6 slices ham
  6 eggs
  2 sprigs green onion, sliced

eggs benedict with roasted asparagus and bolete mushrooms

This classic breakfast dish foregoes the boring (and arguably bland) English muffins in favor of asparagus roasted with earthy bolete mushrooms. Packed with big flavor, this dish will be one your family asks for again and again.

In a high-speed blender or food processor, make the Hollandaise sauce by blending the egg yolks, lemon juice, salt, and cayenne pepper. Add the melted butter at a slow drizzle for 2 minutes. Pour the Hollandaise sauce into a serving dish, and set it aside until it is time to serve it.

For the asparagus and mushrooms, preheat your oven to 400 degrees. Rinse the asparagus under cold water. Break off the tough ends by grabbing them at the base and the top and allowing them to naturally break as you bend them. Place the asparagus in a roasting pan, and toss with the coconut oil, mushrooms, salt, and pepper. Roast at 400 degrees for 35 minutes.

For the eggs Benedict, slice the ham thinly (about 1/4-inch thick). In a large, heavy skillet, sear the ham over medium-high heat. Cook for 3-4 minutes per side until the ham is golden brown on the edges.

Poach the eggs for approximately 5 minutes or until the center is tender but not firm. This will yield a slightly runny yolk. If you're not accustomed to poaching eggs, you can also steam them by cracking them into a skillet over medium heat, adding half cup of water, and covering with a lid. The same test to see if they're done applies, gently poke them at their thickest part to determine the firmness of the yolk.

Plate each dish with roasted asparagus and mushrooms at the bottom, top with a slice of ham, a poached egg, the Hollandaise sauce, and garnish with the sliced green onions.

Serves 6

braised pork belly

No one will ask "where's the bacon" when served this smoky braised pork belly. Tender and juicy, with all the flavors of bacon, this dish will be a hit!

Preheat your oven to 350 degrees. In a small bowl, combine the salt, pepper, onion powder, garlic powder, and smoked paprika. Season the pork belly generously with the spices.

In a roasting pan, place the pork belly fat side up. Surround the pork belly with the carrots and onion. Pour the stock over the vegetables. Cover the roasting pan, and braise for two and a half hours.

Allow the pork belly to cool, and if not serving immediately, place it in the refrigerator. Before serving, allow it to come to room temperature. Then, place it in a 400-degree oven uncovered for 15-20 minutes or until warm and slightly crispy on the top.

Serves 6

1 tablespoon each:
    salt
    black pepper
    onion powder
    garlic powder
    smoked paprika
1 pound pork belly
4 large carrots, chopped
1 large onion, chopped
1 cup chicken stock (see page 290)

sweet potato hash with rosemary

Hash browns have always been a favorite brunch side dish. This roasted sweet potato hash will add color and flavor to your guests' plate, and they will be pleasantly surprised with the hint of rosemary in each bite.

Preheat your oven to 400 degrees. Combine the sweet potatoes with the onion, rosemary, butter, garlic powder, salt, and pepper. Roast uncovered for about 1 hour or until the sweet potatoes are crispy, stirring every 20 minutes.

Serves 6

4 large sweet potatoes, peeled and diced

1 onion, diced

2 tablespoons dried rosemary

2 tablespoons grass-fed butter, melted

1 tablespoon garlic powder

Salt and pepper to taste

1/4 cup coconut flour, sifted

1/4 teaspoon baking soda

1 teaspoon cinnamon

1 tablespoon maple sugar

4 eggs

1 tablespoon water

Melted grass-fed butter for frying

Maple syrup

Cinnamon sticks for garnish

cinnamon maple hot cakes

Nothing says Sunday brunch like warm, buttery pancakes. Cinnamon and maple in the batter add the perfect flavor combination. All you need is a bit of butter on top!

In a medium-sized mixing bowl, combine the coconut flour, baking soda, cinnamon, and maple sugar.

In a separate small mixing bowl, whisk the eggs and water with a fork until frothy. Pour the eggs and water into the dry mixture, and blend with a hand mixer until smooth.

Add melted butter to a hot griddle or skillet, and spoon the batter for each hot cake onto the pan. Cook the hot cakes for 1-2 minutes on each side. Serve with butter and maple syrup, and garnish with a few cinnamon sticks.

Serves 6

springtime tea party

As a child, I (Hayley) had many tea parties with my dolls. I can even remember trying to have a tea party on the bottom of the swimming pool, pretending I was the little mermaid entertaining all of my fishy friends. As you can imagine, that did not go so well.

I actually wasn't too fond of the flavor of tea as a child. Now, as an adult, a tea party is more realistic. It can be a tricky event to coordinate when following a grain-free diet, but with a few modifications, you can make the menu just as tasty and even more fun! A tea party is a great way to spend an afternoon with some of your favorite girlfriends. It's also a lovely theme for a bridal or baby shower, and, of course, it can be a great birthday theme for a little girl.

An invitation to a tea party birthday that includes an invitation for each little girl's favorite doll as the "plus one" is a surefire way to get them excited to spend an afternoon celebrating a friend. For this menu, I got to relive my childhood fantasies of getting all dolled up for a fancy tea party with my cousins and their friends.

We had a lot of fun serving new and old tea party recipes. Scones can easily be made grain-free, and our version of zucchini bread is just as delicious as any traditional recipe. You could serve any of these dishes to skeptical friends, and they wouldn't have a clue that they are all flourless.

Along with a few baked goods, it's good to round out the menu with a few refreshing vegetable dishes. We enjoyed getting creative with our finger foods.

Remember that a tea party is known for having small bites of food and is meant to be a light meal. Don't feel the need to send your friends home with aching bellies. This occasion is a time to chitchat and have a few nibbles here and there.

menu

Rooibos Gingersnap Tea

Cucumber and Salmon Bites

Carrots with Olive Tapenade Trio

Orange Scones and Cranberry Scones

Zucchini Bread

Shopping and Preparation

We were able to find all of our serving ware for this tea party at a local antique shop. You can usually find beautiful tea sets with great character for a low price in such shops.

The fabric store is a great source of simple lace to use as a table runner. Springtime colors of pink and white, soft yellow, and purple are best to style this menu.

Fresh roses and baby's breath make a lovely centerpiece for a tea party, and don't forget the little white gloves!

One day ahead

Today, you can make the scones, zucchini bread, and olive tapenade. Also, stop at your local flower shop for your centerpiece.

Five hours before the party

Set the table. Make sure all of your teacups are dusted and rinsed clean and your silver is polished.

One hour before the party

Put together the carrot slices with the olive tapenade and cucumber bites. Slice the zucchini bread, and set out the scones. Brew the tea, and keep it warm on the stovetop until your guests arrive.

rooibos gingersnap tea

You can't have a tea party without tea, and this rooibos gingersnap is the perfect centerpiece that draws all of the other dishes together. The sweet and tart notes of ginger are nicely complemented by a hint of lemon. Rooibos tea is naturally caffeine-free, so it's fine to serve to children.

Place the tea and candied ginger in a mesh ball. In a kettle on the stove, add the water, and bring it to a boil. Then, pour the boiling water into your teapot, add the mesh ball with tea and ginger, and steep for 4-6 minutes.

Pour the tea into the cups, and serve it with lemon slices and maple sugar cubes.

Serves 4

4 tablespoons loose rooibos tea

1 teaspoon candied ginger

4 cups distilled or spring water

1/2 lemon, sliced thinly

Pure maple sugar cubes

Cucumber and Salmon Bites
- 1 cup salted grass-fed butter, softened
- 1/2 cup chives, minced
- 2 large, seedless cucumbers
- 8 ounces smoked salmon
- Fresh dill for garnish

Olive Tapenade Trio
- 1/2 cup black olives
- 1/2 cup green olives
- 1/2 cup Kalamata olives
- 3/4 cup extra-virgin olive oil
- 3 large carrots
- Chives for garnish

cucumber and salmon bites

We took the classic tea party sandwiches and turned them into adorable, Paleo-friendly appetizers! These refreshing hors d'oeuvres are a beautiful and delicious way to snack during teatime.

In a medium-sized mixing bowl, whip the butter and chives with a hand mixer. Then, refrigerate the chive butter until it's time for plating.

Slice the cucumbers into 1/2-inch pieces. Spread a half teaspoon of chive butter onto each cucumber slice. Top each slice with a small amount of smoked salmon, and garnish each with fresh dill.

Serves 4

carrots with olive tapenade trio

Using a small food processor, pulse the black olives. Add 2-4 tablespoons of olive oil, and continue to process the olives until they turn into a smooth, yet still thick tapenade. Pour the black olive tapenade into a small bowl.

Add the green olives to the food processor, and pulse them as well. Then, add 2-4 tablespoons of olive oil, and continue to process until smooth but thick. Pour the green olive tapenade into a second bowl. Repeat the same process with the Kalamata olives.

Peel the carrots, and slice them at a steep angle to yield 1/2-inch slices. Top each carrot slice with its own spoonful of tapenade, and garnish the carrot with chopped chives. Keep refrigerated until time to serve.

The tapenade can be made up to two days in advance.

Serves 4

Orange Scones

2 cups blanched almond flour

1/4 cup + 2 tablespoons arrowroot flour

1/2 teaspoon salt

2 teaspoons gluten-free baking powder

2 tablespoons pure maple syrup

1/4 cup coconut oil, melted

1 egg

Zest of 1 orange

Cranberry Scones

2 cups blanched almond flour

1/4 cup + 1/8 cup arrowroot flour

1/2 teaspoon salt

2 teaspoons gluten-free baking powder

2 tablespoons pure maple syrup

1/4 cup coconut oil, melted

1 egg

1 cup dried cranberries

orange scones and cranberry scones

Scones are a traditional Scottish bread that is slightly sweet and usually served with tea around the world. For these scones, it's easy to make delicious variations by adding different fruit to the batter. They're wonderful served with apple butter and a hot cup of tea.

Preheat your oven to 350 degrees. In a medium-sized mixing bowl, combine the almond flour, 1/4-cup of arrowroot flour, salt, and baking powder.

In a separate small mixing bowl, combine the maple syrup, melted coconut oil, and egg. Blend with a hand mixer until smooth. Pour the wet ingredients into the dry ingredients, and blend until all ingredients are evenly combined.

To make orange scones, add the orange zest. To make cranberry scones, add the dried cranberries. Add two tablespoons of arrowroot flour to the batter to thicken the dough.

Line a baking sheet with parchment paper, and form the dough into a ball. Place the ball of dough onto the parchment-lined baking sheet, and flatten it slightly. Carefully cut and separate the dough into eight equal wedges, and bake at 350 degrees for 20 minutes.

Serves 8

zucchini bread

These delightful miniature loaves fit the occasion of afternoon tea, yielding perfectly-portioned small slices. They are great served with butter or jam and can also be sliced and toasted for a crispy bite. We love to make these loaves around the holidays as small gifts for family and friends.

1 1/2 cups blanched almond flour

1 tablespoons arrowroot flour

2 teaspoons gluten-free baking powder

1/2 teaspoon salt

1/2 teaspoon cinnamon

1/4 teaspoon nutmeg

2 eggs

1/4 cup pure maple syrup

1/4 cup grass-fed butter, melted

1/2 cup zucchini, shredded

1/2 cup currants

2 mini loaf pans

Preheat your oven to 350 degrees. In a medium-sized mixing bowl, combine the blanched almond flour, arrowroot flour, baking powder, salt, cinnamon, and nutmeg.

In a separate small mixing bowl, combine the eggs, maple syrup, and melted butter, and blend until smooth with a hand mixer. Pour the wet ingredients into the dry ingredients, and continue to blend until the batter is smooth.

Shred the zucchini with a box grater. Place the shredded zucchini in a clean dish towel or paper towel, and squeeze it firmly over a sink or extra bowl to remove the excess water. Stir the shredded zucchini into the batter, along with the currants, until evenly combined.

Pour the batter equally into two parchment-lined mini loaf pans. Bake for 40 minutes at 350 degrees or until a toothpick in the center of the loaf comes out cleanly. Allow to cool before slicing.

Serves 8

easter lunch

Easter marks the beginning of spring for many parts of the country. While it's usually a few weeks before we can safely plant flowers or vegetables outdoors in our area, we celebrate the arrival of warmer weather with great fanfare. At the center of the festivities is Easter lunch. With the change of seasons also comes a burst of color, as we leave the cold and gray days behind us. Flowers emerge from their wintry slumber to dot yards and fields with color. Our typical Easter lunch menu helps to awaken the senses from the long winter hibernation.

In this menu, we place extra special emphasis on incorporating color into the dishes and accompanying decorations. Pastel hues of mint green, canary yellow, robin's egg blue, and soft pink are all part of the color palette for this meal. This colorful menu is sure to brighten up your table and fill plates with delicious flavors.

We had the opportunity to enjoy this special meal with our friends, Henry and Michelle, during a trip to the Bay area of California. The first order of business was to make dyed Easter eggs, which are a must for your centerpiece.

To make your dyed eggs, heat 4 cups of water in a medium saucepan until steam begins to rise. In small mixing bowls, place 2/3 cup hot water with 1 tablespoon of white vinegar. To make dyed eggs, you'll need food coloring. We like using India Tree vegetable based food dyes, because they are natural and derived from vegetables. Add 3-5 drops of food coloring, depending on the shade you desire. If the eggs are not covered with the dye mixture, roll them around frequently to ensure even coloring. Approximately 1-2 minutes is all you need for picture-perfect, pastel-colored eggs. Allow them to dry on overturned egg cartons.

menu

. . . .

Avocado Cream Eggs

Grapefruit Salad

Honey-Glazed Ham

Sweet Potato Soufflé

Roasted Rainbow Carrots

Meyer Lemon Tart

Shopping and Preparation

Fresh greens, tulips, and pastel-colored Easter eggs are a simple and inexpensive way to decorate your table for Easter. White plates make the perfect base for this colorful menu. For an additional pop of color, pick an accent shade from either the dyed eggs or the meal, and use that color for your table napkins.

One day ahead

Make sure you have all the ingredients you need, and grab any last-minute items—a fresh ham, flowers, berries, etc. You can make your soufflé, and keep it refrigerated for the following day. You can also make the lemon tart, prepare the carrots for roasting, boil the eggs for the deviled eggs, and dye the Easter eggs.

Two hours before the meal

Throw together the salad, but save the dressing for right before serving. Bring the ham to room temperature to prepare for baking, and go ahead and roast the carrots.

One hour before the meal

Now, you can bake the ham. As the ham comes to the end of its bake time, warm the roasted carrots and the soufflé. At this point, you are just about ready to serve, so all items should be making their way to the table, and drinks should be poured.

avocado cream eggs

The soft, pale green filling makes for a beautiful twist on classic deviled eggs. The addition of avocado and a hint of crème fraiche add a light flavor and creamy texture to this favorite dish.

In a large saucepan, cover the eggs with water. Bring the water to a boil over medium heat. Once the water starts to boil, set a timer for 10 minutes. When the timer goes off, transfer the eggs into an ice bath. When the eggs are cool, peel them, and slice them in half.

Remove the yolks, and place them in a medium mixing bowl. Add the avocado and crème fraîche, and mash them together with the yolks. Stir in the salt, pepper, garlic powder, and minced chives.

Using a piping bag, fill each egg half with the avocado cream filling. Garnish the deviled eggs with a dusting of paprika and minced chives.

Serves 6

12 eggs, hard boiled and peeled
1 avocado
1 tablespoon crème fraîche
Salt and pepper to taste
1/2 teaspoon garlic powder
1 tablespoon minced chives
Paprika and minced chives for garnish

grapefruit salad

Pink grapefruit and heirloom tomatoes add color and flavor to a simple salad. This whimsical spring salad is quick to make and full of bright, refreshing flavors. Its lightness can be the perfect addition to a meal that includes rich and hearty dishes.

Peel the grapefruit, and carefully slice it to remove the citrus slices from the inner membranes. Toss the salad greens with the grapefruit, tomato, and red onion. Sprinkle the salad with a bit of salt, and drizzle with olive oil and balsamic vinegar.

Serves 6

1 large grapefruit, segmented

5 cups spring mix salad greens

1 medium heirloom tomato, sliced

1/4 medium red onion, julienned

Salt to taste

1/4 cup extra-virgin olive oil

1/8 cup balsamic vinegar

honey-glazed ham

A ham is always fantastic on its own but can be especially lovely with the addition of a simple glaze and a quick roast in the oven. Honey and butter will caramelize over the entire ham, and whole cloves add a wonderful flavor that complements the sweetness of the glaze.

Preheat your oven to 325 degrees. Place the ham in a roasting pan equipped with a roasting rack. Using a pointed knife, lightly pierce the ham at even spacing, and "stud" the ham with the cloves. Pour the apple juice into the roasting pan until it has reached a depth of approximately 1 inch. Bake the ham for about 10 minutes per pound, until it reaches an internal temperature of 160 degrees..

Meanwhile, in a small saucepan, heat the honey and butter until it begins to bubble. Brush the honey glaze over the ham twice while cooking.

Serves 10

5-6 pound cured ham

2 tablespoons whole cloves

4-6 cups pure apple juice

1/2 cup pure honey

1/2 cup grass-fed butter

sweet potato soufflé

A soufflé may seem like an intimidating side dish, but you'll be surprised by how easy it is to make. Take a little bit of extra care to time this dish, though, so that it can be served within moments of coming out of the oven. This will help to prevent the puffed top from subsiding as the steam escapes.

Peel the sweet potatoes, and chop them into 2-inch pieces. Place the sweet potato pieces in a medium saucepan and cover them with water. Bring the water to a boil, and cook until the sweet potatoes are fork tender (about 30-35 minutes). Remove the saucepan from the heat, and drain the water.

Preheat your oven to 350 degrees. Place the boiled sweet potatoes into a high-speed blender or food processor. Add the eggs, butter, coconut milk, maple sugar, baking soda, cinnamon, and salt, and process the mixture until smooth. Pour the mixture into a large soufflé dish, and bake for 45-60 minutes. The soufflé will be done when you can gently shake the dish, and the soufflé is firm but jiggles slightly.

Serves 8

3 large sweet potatoes, peeled and chopped

2 eggs

1/2 cup grass-fed butter

1/4 cup coconut milk

1/2 cup maple sugar

1/2 teaspoon baking soda

1/2 teaspoon cinnamon

1 teaspoon salt

roasted rainbow carrots

Fresh herbs and a hint of cinnamon are a wonderful way to enhance the sweet flavor of roasted carrots. This colorful side dish is a perfect way to celebrate a springtime holiday.

Preheat your oven to 400 degrees. Chop the carrots into 1-inch lengths. Place the carrots in a baking dish. Cut the butter into six equal pieces, and distribute it evenly around the carrots. Dust the carrots with the cinnamon, salt, pepper, and marjoram.

Bake the carrots 45-60 minutes or until fork tender. Garnish the dish with the chopped walnuts, and serve.

Serves 6

2 pounds rainbow carrots

2 tablespoons grass-fed butter

1/2 teaspoon cinnamon

1/2 teaspoon salt

1/2 teaspoon pepper

1 tablespoon fresh marjoram, minced

1/8 cup chopped walnuts

meyer lemon tart

Meyer lemons are a little sweeter in flavor than a typical lemon, almost like a slightly tart orange. Your guests will love the beauty of this dessert and will be sure to ask for seconds!

Preheat your oven to 325 degrees. In a medium-sized bowl, combine the almond flour, salt, and baking soda.

In a separate small mixing bowl, combine the maple syrup and vanilla extract. In a small saucepan, melt the palm oil shortening, and add it to the wet ingredients. Stir the wet ingredients into the dry ingredients, and mix until evenly combined.

Pat the dough into a 9-inch tart pan, and bake for 10-15 minutes or until golden. Remove the crust from the oven to cool.

In a medium-sized mixing bowl, whisk the egg yolks and maple sugar together until smooth. Whisk in the lemon juice and most of the zest. (Reserve some of the zest for garnish.) In a double boiler, heat the mixture, whisking constantly until thick.

Remove the filling from the heat, and whisk in the butter. Pour the filling into the center of the tart crust, and bake for 15 minutes at 325 degrees.

Remove from the oven, allow to cool, and garnish with lemon zest and fresh berries. Refrigerate until serving.

Serves 6

Crust

2 1/2 cups blanched almond flour
1/2 teaspoon salt
1/2 teaspoon baking soda
2 tablespoons pure maple syrup
1 teaspoon pure vanilla extract
1/2 cup palm oil shortening, melted

Filling

5 egg yolks
1/2 cup granulated maple sugar
2 Meyer lemons, zest and juice
1/2 cup grass-fed butter, melted
1/4 cup berries for garnish

backyard picnic

When the days get longer in the spring, there's not much that can keep us indoors. We love spending afternoons with the grass between our toes, digging around in our garden, and going for hikes in the forest. Most of all, we love cooking and eating outdoors.

Whether you plan on enjoying the meal in your backyard or at the top of a local peak, the same rules apply. Try to keep cutting to a minimum so that everything is either bite-sized already or in finger food form. The items should also be able to withstand a few hours without refrigeration. As with any menu, of course, you should consider the balance of flavors and how they all work together.

For this menu, we chose one of our all-time favorite cuts to grill: country-style pork ribs. These perfectly portioned ribs are incredibly flavorful, grill quickly, and make great finger food. The starch of the

No'tato Salad nicely complements the crunch of the fennel slaw and the soft sweetness of the tomato and peach salad. To finish, add some blueberry muffins into the mix, as well as seasonal fresh fruit.

If you do venture into the wilderness, pack a sturdy blanket to sit on. We also filled a mason jar with cucumber-infused lemonade, which was quite refreshing on a hot summer evening. However, no matter where you decide to enjoy this picnic, the flavors of summer will treat you to an unforgettable experience.

menu

. . . .

Teriyaki Country Ribs

No'tato Salad

Creamy Fennel Slaw with Carrots and Apples

Balsamic Tomato and Peach Salad

Lemon Blueberry Muffins

Shopping and Preparation

A picnic is often a spur-of-the-moment type of meal. Pack up leftover food from the night before, whip up some lemonade, and head outside for a relaxing meal in the great outdoors.

One day ahead

Today, you can make the muffins, slaw, and "No'tato Salad." All of these dishes become more delicious when the flavors can marinate overnight. Also set aside anything you might need for the picnic—plates, utensils, and napkins, but also things like a blanket and citronella candles to ward off bugs.

Two hours before the picnic

Grill the ribs, and toss the tomato and peach salad. Gather all of your travel containers, and fill water bottles for traveling.

One hour before the picnic

Pack your basket with plates, silverware, napkins, food, and ice. Grab your blanket, and head to the picnic site.

1/2 cup coconut aminos
1/4 cup brown mustard
5 drops fish sauce
1 clove garlic, pressed
Salt and pepper to taste
3 pounds country-style pork ribs

teriyaki country ribs

Whether you make these at home before hand or cook them over a fire out in the wilderness, these pork ribs are the perfect centerpiece to a picnic in the great outdoors. Take this dish to the next level by lightly smoking the ribs over a fire of lump hickory or apple wood.

Preheat your grill to high heat, or place a griddle over glowing hardwood embers.

Whisk together the coconut aminos and brown mustard in a small mixing bowl. Add in the fish sauce using more or less to taste—it will add a big dose of umami! Press the garlic and whisk into the sauce. Add a dash of salt and pepper to taste.

Place the pork ribs on a hot portion of the grill or griddle and sear for 2 minutes on each side. Move to a cool spot on the grill or reduce heat to medium-low. Brush the pork ribs with the teriyaki sauce. Turn ribs every 3-4 minutes and baste with sauce. Cook 12-15 minutes, until the meat is done to your liking.

Serves 4

10 turnips, boiled
2 hard-boiled eggs
1 cup homemade mayonnaise
    1/3 cup coconut oil, melted
    1/3 cup sesame oil
    1/3 cup extra-virgin olive oil
    1 egg
    1 tablespoon brown mustard
    1 tablespoon lemon juice
    Pinch of salt
1 cup celery, chopped
1/2 cup mayonnaise
2 teaspoons paprika
1 tablespoon fresh chives, chopped
1 tablespoon fresh parsley
2 teaspoons fresh dill
8 ounces ham, cut into chunks
Salt and pepper to taste

no'tato salad

The mild flavor and soft texture of boiled turnips are a great substitution for white potatoes in this classic, creamy salad. Slices of ham add a smoky flavor, and celery provides the perfect crunch.

Fill a large stockpot with water. Cut the ends and tips off of the turnips, and place them in the stockpot. Cover, and boil the turnips over medium heat until fork tender (about 35 minutes).

Once the turnips are fully cooked, remove them from the heat, and drain the water. Allow the turnips to cool completely.

Meanwhile, boil the two eggs by placing them in a small saucepan. Cover them with water, bring to a boil, and allow to boil for ten minutes. Promptly place the hard-boiled eggs in an ice bath and allow to cool completely before peeling.

To make the mayonnaise, melt the coconut oil in a glass liquid measuring cup with a spout. Allow the coconut oil to cool a moment before adding the sesame oil and olive oil. In a food processor or high-speed blender, blend the egg, brown mustard, lemon juice, and a pinch of salt. Drizzle in the oil mixture at a very slow trickle (taking 3-4 minutes for the entire cup of oil). Continue to process the mayonnaise until it has reached the desired consistency.

When the turnips are cool, cut them into bite-sized chunks. Combine the turnips and celery in a large mixing bowl. Gently fold 1/2 cup of mayonnaise into the turnip and celery mixture. Add the paprika, chives, parsley, dill, and ham, and continue to carefully stir all ingredients until combined. Season with salt and pepper to taste.

Chop the hard-boiled eggs, and sprinkle them over the salad. Lightly stir the eggs into the salad, and keep it chilled in the refrigerator until time to serve.

Serves 4

creamy fennel slaw
with carrots and apples

Cole slaw is a classic picnic dish that goes well with just about anything. The apples and fennel are welcome twists that make this creamy slaw stand out from customary versions. Take extra care to consistently julienne the fruits and vegetables, and add a dash of poppy seeds to create a beautiful contrast of colors and textures.

In a small mixing bowl, whisk together the honey and apple cider vinegar. Add a quarter cup of the mayonnaise to the bowl, and continue to whisk. Add a pinch of salt, and whisk again. Keep the creamy dressing refrigerated until use.

In a medium-sized mixing bowl, toss the julienned carrots, fennel bulb, and apple. Add the fennel greens, poppy seeds, salt, and Creamy Slaw Dressing. Toss to combine all ingredients, and chill until time to serve..

Serves 4

Creamy Slaw Dressing
 1 teaspoon honey
 2 tablespoons apple cider vinegar
 1/4 cup homemade mayonnaise (see page 92)
 Pinch of salt

Fennel Slaw
 6 carrots, julienned
 1 fennel bulb, julienned
 1 apple, julienned
 1/4 cup fennel greens, loosely packed, chopped
 1 tablespoon poppy seeds
 Salt to taste

balsamic tomato and peach salad

When you select dishes to take on a picnic, they need to be able to withstand a modest amount of transport. This dish is also great choice to take on a picnic because the tangy notes of the dressing will enhance the flavor of the salad.

Clean and chop the tomatoes and peaches. Roughly chop the cilantro and set aside.

In a medium-sized mixing bowl, combine the tomatoes and peaches. Pour the balsamic vinegar and olive oil over the fruit, sprinkle everything with salt, and top with the chopped cilantro.

Toss the salad to evenly combine, and place in a sealed container for transporting. If desired, you may bring some extra dressing and cilantro to top the salad when you reach your destination.

Serves 4

2 large heirloom tomatoes, cut into chunks

2 large peaches, cut into chunks

3 tablespoons cherry balsamic vinegar

2 tablespoons extra-virgin olive oil

Salt to taste

2 tablespoons fresh cilantro, chopped

lemon blueberry muffins

These tasty muffins are a nice choice for a midsummer picnic when blueberries are in season. With the perfect balance of savory and sweet, they are a welcome treat at the end of a long (or short) hike to your picnic destination.

Preheat your oven to 350 degrees. Place muffin papers into a muffin pan.

In a small mixing bowl, combine the eggs, vanilla extract, maple syrup, and coconut milk. Blend with a hand mixer until smooth.

In a separate medium-sized mixing bowl, combine the coconut flour, salt, baking soda, and lemon zest. Pour the wet mixture into the dry ingredients, and blend with the hand mixture until smooth. Add the melted palm shortening, and continue to blend. Fold the fresh blueberries into the batter, and scoop 1/4 cup of batter into each muffin cup. Bake at 350 degrees for 35 minutes.

Makes 12 muffins

6 eggs

1 teaspoon pure vanilla extract

1/2 cup pure maple syrup

1/4 cup coconut milk

1/2 cup coconut flour, sifted

1 teaspoon salt

1/2 teaspoon baking soda

Zest of half a lemon

1/2 cup palm shortening, melted

2 cups fresh blueberries

a night in tuscany

While in college, I (Bill) had the amazing privilege of studying abroad during the spring semester of my fourth year. (The landscape architecture program at Penn State sends fourth year students to Rome for four months.) I made a point of painting at least once a week, I drank cappuccino at every opportunity, and I ate true Italian cooking almost every night of the week. It was an incredible time.

One side trip particularly stands out from a food standpoint. My classmates and I happened to be in Italy the same time as the winter Olympics were occuring in Torino. On our way to Torino, we spent a night in Milan and went out on the town in search of a great dinner. We eventually settled on a restaurant and ordered pizzas. In Italy, pizzas are much smaller but can still be formidable for the average American appetite. I ordered a Diavola pizza, which is traditionally topped with sort of spicy cured meat like soppressata or capicola, as well as black olives and hot peppers. I finished the entire pizza—still the one and only time I've ever accomplished such a feat.

With this meal, we enjoyed paying tribute to my memories of Italy and bringing a taste of Tuscany to the table for our friends. Though pizza is an American creation, it is now made throughout Italy. Let these recipes take your taste buds on a journey through the Tuscan hills. If you close your eyes, you might even hear the bell towers of San Gimignano.

menu

· ·

Antipasti Salad

Pan-Fried Asparagus

Baked Salmon with Lemon and Capers

Pizza Margherita

Chocolate Chip Biscotti

Affogato with Dark Chocolate Gelato

Shopping and Preparation

For an authentic Italian dinner, gather all of your closest friends to enjoy an evening of food, wine, and laughter. Fresh figs, citrus, and grapes make for a great centerpiece when serving an Italian meal, and candlelight will set the mood for your romantic Tuscan evening.

Soft blues and fresh greens added a lightness to our table setting, and we used a few dishes brought back from Italy to serve the food.

One day ahead

Today, complete all of your produce food shopping. This menu uses a lot of fresh produce and fresh fish, and purchasing it the day before will be your best bet. On this day, you can also make the biscotti, as well as the gelato. Roast the red peppers and marinate them overnight.

Five hours before dinner

At this time, set the table, and prepare and bake the pizza crust. You can toss the salad, leaving dressing for later, and prep the asparagus and fish.

One hour before the party

Put the fish in the oven, and put the pizza in the oven as well to warm with the toppings. You can also pan-fry the asparagus.

As your guests arrive

Dress the salad, and place all of the warm dishes on the table.

Preparing for dessert

As dinner slows down, brew the coffee to have ready for dessert. Enjoy the gelato in a coffee cup with biscotti for dipping as the evening comes to an end.

4 red bell peppers, roasted

1 clove garlic, crushed

2 teaspoons red pepper flakes

2 teaspoons oregano

1 cup extra-virgin olive oil

8 cups romaine lettuce, chopped

1/2 medium red onion, julienned

3/4 cup artichoke hearts

1/3 cup green olives

1/2 cup soppressata, chopped

Dressing

    1 cup extra-virgin olive oil

    1/3 cup balsamic vinegar

    1 tablespoon dried oregano

    1 teaspoon dried basil

    1 teaspoon dried marjoram

    1 teaspoon salt

    1/2 teaspoon black pepper

antipasti salad

This dish, by namesake alone, seems ironic for an Italian meal that does not include pasta. However, this is simply a dish that makes a nice counterpoint to a main course. This salad packs huge flavor and is easy enough to throw together quickly. It'll have your guests saying "molto bene" in no time!

The day before making this salad, place the four red bell peppers on a rimmed baking sheet, and bake them at 450 degrees until the peppers start to develop dark spots on the skin (about 25-30 minutes). Rotate the peppers to blacken them evenly. Remove them from the oven, and allow them to cool. Then, peel the skin away, remove the seeds, and cut into strips.

Place the cleaned pepper strips in a small mason jar. Add the crushed garlic, red pepper flakes, oregano, and olive oil to the jar, and refrigerate overnight.

The next day, in a large serving bowl, toss the chopped romaine lettuce, red onion, roasted red pepper mixture from the jar, artichoke hearts, green olives, and soppressata.

In a separate mixing bowl, whisk together the dressing ingredients—olive oil, balsamic vinegar, oregano, basil, marjoram, salt, and black pepper. Toss with the salad to combine.

Serves 4

pan-fried asparagus

We love to make pan-fried asparagus for a quick and easy side dish, as it accompanies an Italian meal very well. This dish comes together beautifully with the pop of flavor and color from the yellow cherry tomatoes.

In a cast iron skillet over medium heat, heat the butter. Rinse the asparagus, and chop the bunch about a third of the way up from the ends. Discard the stalks.

Mince the garlic, and set it aside.

Add the asparagus to the skillet, and sauté it until tender (about 10 minutes). Add the minced garlic, along with the salt and pepper. Finally, add the cherry tomatoes and sauté for another 5 minutes. Serve.

Serves 8

1 tablespoon grass-fed butter

2 pounds asparagus

2 cloves garlic, minced

Salt and pepper to taste

1/2 cup cherry tomatoes

3 pounds salmon fillets

2 tablespoons grass-fed butter

1/8 cup capers

1 lemon, sliced

Salt and pepper to taste

baked salmon with lemon and capers

When you hear "Italian food," you may first think of pasta, but don't forget the fantastic flavors of seafood in Italy. Capers and lemons add a fresh flavor to this simply baked salmon, making this dish the perfect addition to a hearty Italian meal.

Preheat your oven to 350 degrees. Rinse the salmon under cool water, and pat it dry. Place pats of butter down the center of the fillets. Sprinkle them with capers, and garnish them with lemon slices. Bake the salmon for 15 minutes per pound for a total of 45 minutes. Add salt and pepper to taste, and serve.

Serves 8

pizza margherita

Even the pickiest child will go back for seconds with this grain-free version of a classic Margherita pizza. The seasoned crust has just the right amount of crunch and crumble, and the warm cheese and basil topping will have your mouth watering as it comes piping hot out of the oven.

Preheat the oven to 325 degrees. In a large mixing bowl, combine all of the crust ingredients—almond flour, arrowroot flour, baking powder, salt, black pepper, oregano, basil, marjoram, garlic powder, onion powder, coconut oil, and eggs. Mix thoroughly until a dough forms. Roll the dough into a ball, and place it on a parchment-lined baking sheet. Flatten the dough to a consistent thickness of 1/4-inch, forming it into a rectangle or circle, depending on your preference. Bake the dough for 20 minutes until it becomes a firm crust.

While the crust is baking, make the sauce. In a medium saucepan, heat the fire-roasted tomatoes and tomato paste over medium heat. Add the pressed garlic, minced onion, oregano, basil, salt, and pepper. Stir to combine, and let the sauce simmer while the crust is cooking.

When the crust is done, smooth a small portion of the sauce on the pizza, using more or less depending on your preference. Less sauce will yield a more crispy pizza, and more sauce will yield a softer pizza. Be careful, however, as too much sauce will make it impossible to pick up the pieces. Add the mozzarella, tomato, and basil toppings on top of the sauce, and bake the pizza for an additional 20 minutes. Turn up the heat to 400 degrees after 20 minutes, and cook for a final 5 minutes.

Serves 6

Crust

2 cups blanched almond flour

1/2 cup arrowroot flour

2 teaspoons gluten-free baking powder

1 teaspoon salt

1 teaspoon black pepper

2 teaspoons dried oregano

1 teaspoon dried basil

1 teaspoon dried marjoram

1 teaspoon garlic powder

1 teaspoon onion powder

1/4 cup coconut oil, melted

2 eggs

Sauce

14 ounces crushed, fire-roasted tomatoes

6 ounces tomato paste

1 clove garlic, pressed

2 tablespoons finely minced onion

1 teaspoon dried oregano

1 teaspoon dried basil

Salt and pepper to taste

Toppings

1/2 cup buffalo mozzarella

1 medium tomato, thinly sliced

10 basil leaves

2 cups blanched almond flour

1/3 cup + 1 tablespoon arrowroot flour

2 teaspoons gluten-free baking powder

1/2 teaspoon salt

1 egg

1/3 cup pure maple syrup

1 teaspoon pure vanilla extract

1 cup dark chocolate chips

2 tablespoons palm shortening

chocolate chip biscotti

This decadent recipe for chocolate chip biscotti will have you second guessing every bite. Did you really use almond flour to make this treat? Enjoy this Italian biscuit with the perfect scoop of gelato for a tasty twist on biscotti and coffee.

Preheat your oven to 350 degrees. In a medium-sized mixing bowl, combine the almond flour, 1/3 cup of the arrowroot flour, baking powder, and salt.

In a separate smaller mixing bowl, combine the egg, maple syrup, and vanilla extract. Using a hand mixer, blend the wet ingredients until evenly combined. Pour the wet ingredients into the dry ingredients, and blend until smooth. Stir in 1/2 cup of the dark chocolate chips. Then, add the remaining one tablespoon of arrowroot flour to firm up the batter.

Line a baking sheet with parchment paper. Roll the dough into a ball, and place it on the parchment-lined baking sheet. Flatten the ball into a 1-inch thick, slightly domed, rectangular shape. Bake the dough for fifteen minutes at 350 degrees.

Allow the dough to cool slightly. Then, using a long knife, cut it very carefully into 1-inch-wide cookies. The cookies will be fragile at this point, so take extra care with them. You can separate them using a careful sweeping motion with the knife.

Bake for an additional 20 minutes at 350 degrees. Reduce the temperature to 250 degrees, and bake for 20 more minutes. This will bring the total cooking time to 55 minutes. Melt the remaining 1/2 cup of dark chocolate chips over a double boiler with the palm shortening. Drizzle the chocolate ganache over the biscotti, allow to harden and serve.

Serves 8

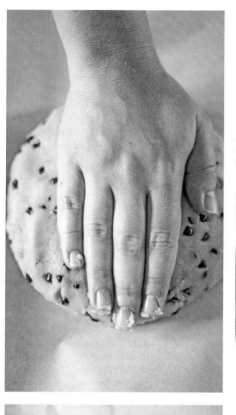

Gelato

16 fluid ounces coconut milk, full fat

1 teaspoon pure vanilla extract

1/4 cup maple syrup

3 egg yolks

1/4 cup cocoa powder

Affogato

1/4 cup ground coffee

1 1/2 cups water

This dish would work well with a shot of espresso in place of the coffee.

Affogato with Dark Chocolate Gelato

Every great Italian meal requires an indulgent dessert, and this one ties together many Italian flavors in one delicious dish. During my time living in Rome, my friends and I often took a walk for gelato after a meal, so it makes the perfect ending for this menu.

In a medium-sized saucepan, combine the coconut milk, vanilla extract, maple syrup, egg yolks, and cocoa powder. Bring the mixture to a low boil while whisking. Then, let it cool.

Strain the mixture into a medium mixing bowl, and cover it with plastic wrap. Chill it in a refrigerator for two hours.

Then, pour the mixture into an ice cream maker, and process it until the desired consistency is reached. Keep the gelato frozen until a few minutes before serving.

To make the affogato, in a French press, cover the ground coffee with 1 1/2 cups of boiling water. Allow the coffee to brew for 3-5 minutes (a longer brewing time will generally yield stronger flavor). Slowly depress the plunger to separate the coffee from the grinds.

Place a scoop of the dark chocolate gelato in a small bowl, and pour 1-2 ounces of the hot coffee over the top. Serve immediately.

Serves 8

midsummer garden party

Summer here in Western Pennsylvania is glorious. After enduring five to six months of dreary, cold, and snowy weather, the warmer months are truly appreciated. This year, we had a particularly hot summer, but also received an abundance of rain early on. This led to what could only be described as epic gardening conditions.

Our vegetable garden took on a mind of its own and sprawled out past its borders, all but preventing us from passing. We grew six different varieties of tomatoes, bibb lettuce, green and red bell peppers, pickling cucumbers, green beans, strawberries, at least ten different types of culinary herbs, broccoli, cauliflower, and even sweet potatoes … and that was just in our 10' x 15' plot. We also experimented with several plants in containers on our back porch. While those didn't turn out so well, the raised bed produced heavily.

Our passion for gardening grew long before we met one another, from seeds planted by our parents. Hayley's grandmother is a master gardener, and she passed that love along to her father who grows pickle-perfect cucumbers every year. In my (Bill's) family, my mother was the one to foster my passion for gardening early on. I can still remember her taking me to the nursery at age ten to pick out a plant for myself. I chose a hosta, which has been divided many times over in the last twenty years.

The summers of my teen years were spent gardening alongside my mother, and then starting my own small landscaping company. I loved my time outdoors, getting my hands dirty and helping people make their yards beautiful. I went on to study landscape architecture at Penn State, and ultimately become a registered landscape architect.

We planned our midsummer garden party at my parents house across town. It was a nice opportunity to get family and friends together to enjoy a warm summer evening with great food and the scenery I had worked to create alongside my mother for the better part of a decade.

menu

· ·

Watermelon Salad with Mint

Bacon-Wrapped Shrimp

Pan-Seared Chicken with Onions
and Mushrooms

Grilled Balsamic Vegetables

Green Bean Salad with Artichoke Hearts
and Olives

Apple Pie with Lattice Crust

Shopping and Preparation

Five days ahead

Prepare the table settings, and select a color theme. Look for wild growing flowers, as well as fresh vegetables for the centerpiece. Review your shopping list, and make note of all of the ingredients that you already have at home. Iron any linens, and neatly fold them so that they're ready to go when you need them.

Three days ahead

Go to the market for all of the items on your shopping list. Purchase extra colorful vegetables for the table decorations if you don't have veggies growing outside.

One day ahead

Make the apple pie filling. Keep the filling in the refrigerator until the following day. At this point you can also make the dressing for the green bean salad, and keep it chilled until use.

Three hours before the party

Bake the apple pie. Prepare all of the veggies for the grill, and steam the green beans. Once the green beans have cooled, toss them with olives and artichoke hearts, and refrigerate them until just before serving. You can now cut the watermelon to have it ready for plating.

One hour before the party

Grill the veggies, and put the shrimp in the oven. You can now plate the watermelon salad, and keep it chilled until your guests arrive. At this point, you can also pan-sear the chicken, and sauté the onions and garlic. Cover it with foil until baking.

Fifteen minutes before your guests arrive

Plate the shrimp and the grilled veggies. Once the veggies are plated, cover them with foil to keep them warm. Place the chicken dish in the oven to bake for 30 minutes. Now, you can place berries in each guest's wine glass.

As your guests arrive

Serve the appetizers and the wine with berries. Once the chicken is finished baking, remove it from the oven, and cover it with foil to keep it warm.

After dinner is over, as your guests are relaxing and enjoying themselves, put the pie in the oven at 350 degrees to warm it. Once the pie is warm, whip the cream for serving.

watermelon salad with mint

This appetizer is perfect for a summer garden party, with its refreshing flavors. Your guests will be pleasantly surprised by the unexpected complimentary flavors of watermelon, lemon, and mint.

Slice the watermelon into 1-inch cubes, removing the rind and any seeds. Rinse, and roughly chop the mint. Arrange the watermelon on a large platter with the mint throughout the dish. Drizzle the watermelon and mint with the lemon juice, and sprinkle it with salt. Serve the salad with toothpicks so that your guests can easily pick up and enjoy it as an appetizer.

Serves 8

Watermelon Salad

    1/2 seedless watermelon, cubed
    1/2 cup fresh mint leaves, julienned
    Juice of 1/2 lemon
    1 teaspoon salt

bacon-wrapped shrimp

Bacon-wrapped Shrimp

    1 1/2 pounds raw shrimp, peeled, tail-on
    18 ounces nitrate-free bacon

When you're entertaining, you need a mixture of dishes that are elegant and impressive, as well as dishes that are delicious but easy to execute. There's nothing complicated about this dish, but boy, is it a crowd-pleaser. During our party, these simple bacon-wrapped shrimp skewers received rave reviews.

Cut the strips of bacon in half. Wrap the shrimp, starting from the head and working toward the tail. Skewer each shrimp with a 4-inch toothpick.

Preheat your oven to 350 degrees. Place the skewered shrimp on parchment-lined baking sheets. Cook for 30 minutes until the bacon is crisp and the shrimp is opaque.

Serves 8

2 tablespoons grass-fed butter

18 boneless, skinless chicken thighs

Salt and pepper to taste

3 cups sliced white mushrooms

1 yellow onion, thinly sliced

1 bunch fresh thyme leaves

pan-seared chicken
with onions and mushrooms

Boneless chicken thighs are wonderful in this recipe, but you could easily use any part of the chicken you desire. The juices of the onion and mushrooms create a simple sauce as the chicken releases juices of its own while roasting. It is truly divine!

Preheat your oven to 350 degrees. In a large skillet, melt the butter over medium-high heat. Sear the chicken thighs for 2 minutes per side, and sprinkle them with salt and pepper. Add more butter for new batches of thighs as needed. When the chicken thighs are seared, place them in a large baking dish, and set them aside.

Sauté the mushrooms and onion in the same pan used for the chicken until the onion is translucent. Pour the mushrooms and onion over the chicken thighs. Sprinkle the dish with the fresh thyme leaves, and bake for 30 minutes.

Serves 8

grilled balsamic vegetables

When you bring a large group together for dinner, there are bound to be different taste preferences from person to person. For such an occasion, we like to provide a variety of vegetables for people to enjoy. This dish is a sure winner with the variety of colors, textures, and tastes it offers.

Heat a grill to medium-high heat. In a large bowl, toss the peppers, carrots, eggplant, onion, mushrooms, zucchini squash, and yellow squash with the balsamic vinegar, macadamia nut oil, oregano, basil, salt, and pepper.

Grill the vegetables in a grill basket or on a fish plate for 10-15 minutes, flipping as needed. Serve hot, arranged by vegetable.

Serves 8

3 bell peppers, chopped

4 large carrots, peeled and cut into large slices

1 eggplant, sliced

1 red onion, sliced

2 Portobello mushrooms, cut lengthwise

2 zucchini squash, cut lengthwise

2 yellow squash, cut lengthwise

1/2 cup balsamic vinegar

1/2 cup macadamia nut oil

1 tablespoon dried oregano

1 tablespoon dried basil

1 teaspoon salt

1 teaspoon black pepper

green bean salad with artichoke hearts and olives

We like to get our food from places as close to the kitchen as possible. My mother plants a wonderful vegetable garden every year, with green beans as a staple crop. In light of the dinner theme, we picked green beans from the garden for this dish the same day of the meal.

In a large pot, steam the green beans until they are fork tender (about 10 minutes). Allow the green beans to cool completely. Then, pour them into a serving dish, and toss them with the olives and artichoke hearts.

In a small mixing bowl, whisk together the olive oil, lemon juice, oregano, basil, salt, and pepper. Pour the dressing over the green bean salad, and serve.

Serves 8

2 pounds fresh green beans, steamed

1 can black olives

1 can artichoke hearts,
    drained and rinsed with water

1/4 cup extra-virgin olive oil

Juice of 1 lemon

1 teaspoon dried oregano

1 teaspoon dried basil

Pinch of salt

1/2 teaspoon black pepper

apple pie with lattice crust

My parents have an old Macintosh apple tree at their house, and we spent the evening before the party picking apples for this pie. The lattice crust takes some patience, but the payoff is worth it.

To make the filling, melt the butter in a large soup pot over medium heat. Add the apples to the pot, and stir to make sure they are evenly coated with butter. Add the lemon juice, maple syrup, cinnamon, and nutmeg, and continue to cook, stirring as needed until the apples have started to cook down slightly and soften. Transfer the filling to a glass container, and allow to cool. Once cool, refrigerate until use.

Preheat your oven to 325 degrees, and prepare to make the crust and lattice crust dough. In a medium mixing bowl, combine the almond flour, arrowroot flour, salt, baking soda, and maple sugar. Once combined, add the vanilla extract and palm shortening. Then, add the whisked eggs, and stir. Make a ball out of the dough, and dust it with additional arrowroot flour.

Lay out parchment paper on a large cutting board, and dust it with arrowroot flour. Place the dough onto the parchment paper, cover it with another sheet of parchment paper, and roll it out to 1/4-inch thickness. Place the pie pan upside down on the rolled out dough, and using a dull knife, score around the rim of the pan leaving half an inch of extra dough. Remove the excess dough and reserve for the lattice crust. Carefully flip the pan with the dough, allowing the dough to sink into the pie pan as it flips. If necessary, use the extra dough to fix any mishaps or to create a more decorative edge.

Bake the crust for 15 minutes. While the crust is baking, roll out the remaining dough using the same method. Use a pizza cutter or knife to cut 3/4-inch-wide strips of dough for the lattice, setting it aside until the crust has finished baking.

Remove the crust from the oven, and fill it with the apple filling. Place the strips of crust along the top of the pie going in one direction, followed by an additional layer of crust going in the opposite direction to create a classic lattice crust. Brush the lattice crust with the egg white, and bake 15-20 minutes or until golden brown.

Makes one 9-inch pie
Serves 10

Filling

2 tablespoons grass-fed butter

5 medium apples, cored
and sliced to 1/4-inch thickness

1/2 tablespoon lemon juice

1/4 cup pure maple syrup

1 teaspoon ground cinnamon

1/4 teaspoon freshly grated nutmeg

Crust and Lattice

3 cups blanched almond flour

1 cup arrowroot flour + extra for dusting

1 teaspoon salt

1 teaspoon baking soda

1/4 cup maple sugar

1 tablespoon pure vanilla extract

1/2 cup palm shortening, melted

2 eggs, whisked

1 egg white

tropical getaway

Life in the tropics is something only the lucky among us get to experience on a daily basis. For most, a getaway to the islands is a rare vacation enjoyed once every few years (if ever), and we just whimsically daydream it about during the cooler months of the year.

To celebrate ten years of marriage, our friend, Erin, and her husband invited us to Kamalame Cay, a sun-kissed strip of land just off the east coast of Andros Island in the Bahamas. Of course, we could not pass up an opportunity like that and excitedly marked the week in mid-October on our calendar.

In the Bahamas, October is considered "shoulder season"—not quite the low tourist season of summer and not quite the high season of winter. On our second to last night on the Cay, we planned to bring a few friends together at the home of Brian and Jennifer Hew, the owners of the resort, and enjoy a luxurious meal. Luckily, we were able to get some amazingly fresh seafood the day of our dinner. The setting could not have been more gorgeous. We set the table beneath swaying palm trees just a few yards from their private beach. We served dinner at sunset, as the sky turned gorgeous shades of pink and purple. Even though the food didn't last long, we all remained around the table long into the night as the amazing stars came out.

This meal is sure to bring the flavors of the tropics to your home, no matter what time of year it is! Even if you don't live on an island, these dishes will help you escape to a far away place with cool breezes and warm sunshine. Sit back, relax, and get some sand between your toes.

menu

· ·

Micro-Greens Salad with Diced Mango

Stuffed Red Snapper

Spiny Lobster Tails with Drawn Butter

Fried Plantains with Mango Salsa

Shopping and Preparation

You don't need to be beachside to make your guests feel as though they're relaxing on a tropical island. All you need are some big palms, which are terrific outdoor plants that will make you feel like you're on a tropical island all summer long. We always have some palms sitting on our back deck during the warm months. Just bring them inside when it starts to get cold again, and you will have them for years.

Tropical island music will also set the mood during a summer feast. Nothing says relaxation like some steel drums and a fruity cocktail.

Three days ahead

If you don't have tropical-themed effects, now is the time to shop. Try to get fresh coconuts, tropical plants (or leaves), and vibrant table linens.

One day ahead

Gather your produce, and purchase your fish if you aren't near a local fish market. You can also make the mango salsa so that the flavors can marinate overnight.

The day of the party

If you are close to a fresh fish market, purchase your fish and lobster tails. Decorate for the party, and make sure that you are set up with lots of island music to play. As your guests arrive, serve them a fruity drink, and encourage them to mingle before dinner.

micro-greens salad with diced mango

Chef Ricardo at the Cay uses micro-greens in many dishes that he prepares. Not only do they taste great and provide interesting texture, but they also serve as a beautiful garnish. This salad is refreshing with cool crisp lettuce, sweet chunks of mango, and a bright and balanced dressing of lemon and olive oil. It's the perfect salad after a day of scuba diving or reef fishing.

Place micro-greens in a large salad bowl. Top the greens with the mango, red onion, carrot, and cherry tomatoes. Squeeze the lemon juice over the salad, drizzle with olive oil, and season it with salt. Toss to combine, and serve.

Serves 8

5 cups micro-greens

1/2 mango, chopped

1/8 cup red onion, thinly sliced

1 carrot, sliced into ribbons

6 cherry tomatoes, quartered

Juice of 1/2 lemon

2 tablespoons extra-virgin olive oil

Salt to taste

stuffed red snapper

Seafood is central to Bahamian cooking, and red snapper is a commonly caught fish. We enjoyed snapper several nights during our time on the Cay and were lucky enough to get a few freshly caught ones for our big dinner. Our original intent was to go out and catch the fish ourselves, but rough seas ahead of a tropical storm made us think it would be best to leave the fishing to the professionals.

Preheat your oven to 375 degrees on convection setting, if possible. Rinse the snapper under cool water, and pat dry, including the body cavity. Rub the snapper with butter, including the body cavity.

In a small bowl, combine the sea salt, ground sage, and black pepper, and generously sprinkle the fish with the seasoning mixture. Stuff each fish with a heaping handful of rosemary, two garlic cloves per fish, and 3 lemon slices. Bake for 30-35 minutes, and serve.

Serves 8

4 whole red snapper fish
   (about 1 1/2 pounds each)
3 tablespoons grass-fed butter
1 tablespoon sea salt
1 tablespoon ground sage
1 tablespoon black pepper
5 sprigs fresh rosemary
8 garlic cloves, smashed
2 lemons, thinly sliced

6 warm-water lobster tails

1/2 cup grass-fed butter, melted

2 lemons, cut into wedges

spiny lobster tails with drawn butter

Warm water lobsters, also known as spiny lobsters, are primarily sought after for their tails. The reason for that is simple: Their claws are far smaller than their northern cold water cousins. Diving for lobsters is a large part of the local fishing industry in the Bahamas, and as a result, we were able to get these fresh tails the day of our dinner. Lobster is one of those dishes that you can dress up in a million ways, but it's best when served simply. We chose to prepare ours with the classic island approach of less is more.

In a large stockpot, cover the lobster tails with water. Cover the stockpot with a lid, and turn the burner to medium heat. Bring the lobster tails to a boil, and continue to boil until the shells are pink and the lobster is no longer translucent (about 20 minutes).

In a small saucepan, warm the butter until melted. Serve the lobster alongside the drawn butter and fresh lemon wedges.

Serves 8

fried plantains with mango salsa

Fried plantains are a staple starchy food throughout Central America, the Caribbean islands, and equatorial Africa. Botanically similar to bananas (which are sometimes called "dessert bananas" in other parts of the world to separate them from plantains), plantains are starchier and can have varying levels of sweetness. That sweetness can readily be determined by their firmness and color. For this recipe, select green plantains that are somewhat firm.

Mango Salsa

    1 mango

    1/4 red onion

    1 green bell pepper

    1/4 cup tomatoes

    1 garlic clove, minced

    1/8 cup extra-virgin olive oil

    Juice of 2 limes

    2 teaspoon salt

1/2 cup lard

5 green plantains

Salt to taste

To make the mango salsa, peel the skin off the mango, and finely dice the meat. Finely dice the red onion. Remove the seeds from the green bell pepper and tomatoes, and finely dice them as well. In a medium-sized bowl, toss these ingredients together. Add the minced garlic, olive oil, lime juice, and salt. Stir to combine all ingredients, and chill until time to serve.

Heat a cast iron skillet over medium-high heat. Add the lard to the skillet to heat for frying. Peel the plantains, and cut them into large 1-inch chunks. Place the plantain pieces in the skillet, and fry them on each side until golden brown.

Remove the plantains from the skillet, and press down each plantain with a ramekin or flat-bottomed bowl to create a small pancake. Fry the plantains again for 1 minute per side.

Remove the plantains from the skillet, and sprinkle them with salt. Serve them topped with the mango salsa.

Serves 8

a taste of cuba

In the early stages of planning dinners with our friends for this book, we got a generous offer from Chuck and Tracy, who are friends with Hayley's aunt and uncle. This couple has a beautiful house in southern Florida, and they invited us for a long weekend of fishing. Who in the world could refuse?

It was nice to detach from the hustle and bustle of life up north for a few days while we enjoyed the company of family and friends in the warm Florida sun. Of course, the highlight of the trip was a day fishing on the open waters off the coast. Chuck took several of us out on his boat, and on our way to the reef, we set out lines behind the boat in hopes of hooking a Mahi Mahi or two. A few minutes in, one of the lines started buzzing, and before we knew it, there was a gorgeous Mahi Mahi. When we got to the reef, the action heated up. I (Bill) caught a pair of ocean perch, and others caught yellow tail snappers, and a few other types of fish.

Meanwhile, Hayley was back at the house preparing dinner. She wasn't particularly interested in the day's adventures on the high seas, so she set about creating a feast for all to enjoy. Southern Florida is a mixture of cultures and foods, but nothing is more prominent than Cuban food. We wanted to give everyone a true taste of Cuba, so we selected several popular dishes.

While this meal certainly brings an exotic flavor to the table, the ingredients are found in most grocery stores. At the core of authentic Cuban food is the commitment to using only the freshest ingredients. When you recreate this dinner, ask your fishmonger to recommend his freshest, wild caught white fish (it doesn't have to be Wahoo). We had an amazing weekend at Chuck and Tracy's house, and this meal was the perfect ending to our wonderful time.

menu

Yuca con Mojo
(Yuca with Garlic Sauce)

Costillitas
(Cuban Baby Back Ribs)

Pescados Asado
(Grilled Fish)

Arroz Azafrán
(Saffron Rice)

Flan de Coco
(Coconut Flan)

Shopping and Preparation

A Florida vacation is the perfect opportunity to enjoy a classic Cuban meal. There is a great deal of fresh citrus used in Cuban cooking, which adds refreshing flavors to the dishes. Most dishes require little seasoning, with most of the flavor coming from the fresh meat and fish, as well as lemons, limes, and herbs.

We really enjoyed serving a classic Cuban flan to our guests and were thrilled to hear that it was considered to be "better than real Cuban flan" from a guest who is local to Florida.

For this menu, we let the tropical scenery of Florida do the talking on our table setting. We purchased a few tropical plants as our centerpiece, and left the rest to Mother Nature's beautiful outdoors!

One day ahead

If this meal is being prepared while on vacation, you may not have the freedom to do a lot of shopping prior to the dinner. You will be using simple and fresh ingredients for this menu, so you can purchase all items the day before. Collect seashells from the beach to decorate the table, and add tropical fruits and plants. Tonight, make the flan, and keep it in the refrigerator overnight.

The day of the meal

The morning of your dinner is a great time to get a lot of your prep work done. Create the table settings. Grate your cauliflower for a quick cook time, and marinate the ribs. You can also peel and cut your yuca so they are ready to boil when needed.

One hour before dinner

This will be your time to marinate the fish. You don't want to leave fish in citrus too long, or it will start to cook. A quick citrus marinate for fish is all you need, and save the extra juices for basting during grilling.

yuca con mojo
(yuca with garlic sauce)

Cassava, also known as yuca, is a starchy tuber that can be used in place of white potatoes in a recipe. This tasty Cuban dish, Yuca con Mojo, is boiled yuca tossed with a dressing of garlic, onion, and citrus.

2 pounds yuca

1/2 cup grass-fed butter

3 cloves garlic, minced

1 large yellow onion, chopped

Juice of 2 limes

1/3 cup lemon juice (about 3 lemons)

Salt and pepper to taste

Parsley for garnish

Peel the yuca, cut it in half lengthwise, and cut it into 2-3-inch pieces. In a large soup pot, cover the yuca with water. Cover the pot with a lid, and turn the burner to medium-high heat. Bring the water to a boil, and turn the heat down to medium-low. Allow the water to bubble until the yuca is fork tender (about 30 minutes).

Drain the yuca in a colander, and allow it to cool. While the yuca is cooling, prepare the sauce. Heat a large skillet over medium heat. Add one tablespoon of the butter to the skillet. When the butter is hot, add the minced garlic and onion. Sauté until the onion is translucent (about 5 minutes). Add the remaining butter, lime juice, and lemon juice. Season with salt and pepper to taste, and stir. Turn the heat down to low, and simmer for 10 minutes.

Once the yuca is cool to the touch, remove the fibrous center from each piece. Place the yuca in the skillet, and toss it with the garlic sauce. Place the yuca in the skillet, and toss it with the garlic sauce.

Serves 8

2 racks baby back pork ribs

8 cloves garlic, pressed

Juice of 3 large lemons

Juice of 1 orange

Juice of 1 lime

1/4 teaspoon dried oregano

1 tablespoon salt

costillitas (cuban baby back ribs)

A Cuban marinade of orange juice and herbs is a light, refreshing way to enjoy ribs. The orange juice caramelizes on the grill, creating a tangy yet sweet sauce, but you will still be able to taste the citrus when you take that first bite.

Cut each rack of ribs in half, rinse them thoroughly under cold water, and pat them dry.

In a medium-sized mixing bowl, add the pressed garlic, lemon juice, orange juice, lime juice, oregano, and salt. Whisk until combined.

Place the ribs in a large container, and pour the marinade over the ribs, making sure that all ribs are covered evenly. Cover the ribs, and refrigerate them for 2-3 hours.

Just before cooking, preheat your grill to medium-high heat. Place the ribs on the hot grate, and sear for 2-3 minutes on each side. Reduce the heat to low, and continue to cook for 15-20 minutes. The grill temperature should be about 300 degrees. The ribs will be done when they reach an internal temperature of 165 degrees when measured with a meat thermometer.

Slice the ribs, and serve them over greens.

Serves 8

3 pounds wahoo* (white fish)

1/2 cup macadamia nut oil

Juice of 1 lemon

Juice of 1 lime

6 cloves garlic, crushed and minced

1/4 cup cilantro, chopped

3 scallions, chopped

2 teaspoons red pepper flakes

Salt and pepper to taste

pescados asado (grilled fish)

Pescados asado is a fantastic way to prepare meaty cuts of fish. We used freshly caught wahoo, which is a sturdy white fish. A bite of wahoo will have you convinced you have just eaten chicken, the ideal fish to serve any friend who may not be too keen on seafood.

In a medium-sized mixing bowl, add the macadamia nut oil, lemon juice, lime juice, garlic, cilantro, scallions, red pepper flakes, and salt and pepper to taste. Whisk until combined.

In a shallow pan, place the fish, and cover it with marinade. Cover the pan, and put it in the refrigerator for up to 2 hours but no longer.

Just before grilling, preheat your grill to medium heat. Place the fish on the grill at a generous spacing so that each can cook evenly and be flipped with ease. The wahoo will take approximately 5 minutes per side to cook. You will know it's ready to be flipped when it releases easily and cleanly from the grill. Use a wide, flexible spatula to flip the fish. It will be done when it flakes easily and is opaque throughout.

Serves 8

* If you cannot find wahoo, you can use another type of fish, such as salmon, snapper, mahi mahi, halibut, or cod.

3 heads yellow cauliflower, grated

1 red bell pepper

1 green bell pepper

1 yellow onion

8 strands of saffron

3 tablespoons coconut oil

Salt and pepper to taste

Flat-leaf parsley for garnish

arroz azafrán (saffron rice)

What would Cuban food be without rice and beans? For this menu, we held the beans and the rice but still enjoyed the flavors of Spanish rice by using grated cauliflower in its place. We had all of our guests fooled that this was real rice, and they loved every bite!

Rinse the cauliflower under cold water, and pat it dry. Using a box grater, carefully grate the cauliflower florets into a rice-like texture. Place the grated cauliflower into a large mixing bowl.

Dice the bell pepper and onion, and place them in a medium-sized mixing bowl. Refrigerate the vegetables until cooking time.

Crush the saffron strands using a mortar and pestle. Place the crushed saffron in a small mixing bowl, and cover it with hot water to dissolve it.

In a large skillet, heat one tablespoon of coconut oil over medium heat. Add the onion and bell pepper to the skillet, and sauté them until tender (about 5 minutes). Add another tablespoon of coconut oil to the skillet, and continue to sauté the onion and peppers. Add the saffron-infused water to the skillet, and sauté the onion and pepper until all of the water evaporates. Add the cauliflower to the skillet, season with salt and pepper to taste, and lightly sauté until the cauliflower is tender but not soft. Garnish with the chopped parsley, and serve with your favorite hot sauce.

Serves 8

flan de coco (coconut flan)

Flan is a classic Spanish custard that's similar to crème brulée except the caramel cooks along with the custard instead of a sugar crust broiled on top. This results in warm, liquid caramel spilling over the dish when you transfer the dessert to a cake stand. A mouth-watering delight!

3/4 cup maple sugar

3 whole eggs + 5 egg yolks

1 3/4 cups coconut milk

1 cup heavy whipping cream

3 tablespoons dark coconut rum

Shredded coconut for topping

Caramel Sauce

    3 tablespoons grass-fed butter

    3/4 cup maple sugar

Preheat your oven to 325 degrees. In a large mixing bowl, whisk together the maple sugar, eggs, and egg yolks. Add the coconut milk, heavy cream, and rum to the bowl, and continue to whisk until smooth.

In a heavy saucepan, make the caramel sauce by melting the butter and maple sugar over low heat. Once the maple sugar has started to dissolve, pour the mixture into the bottom of an 8-inch soufflé dish or cake pan. Spread the sugar mixture evenly over the bottom of the pan. It will still be semi-solid, so you will need to work with it to spread it on the pan. Pour the flan batter into the baking dish slowly.

Fill a large roasting pan (one that can fit the soufflé dish within it) with about 1-inch of water. Place the soufflé dish into the water bath, and bake it for 45-60 minutes or until the flan is set.

Allow the flan to cool for 5 minutes. Then, release the edges gently with a dull knife. Refrigerate the flan overnight.

Before plating the flan, run a dull knife along the edge again to ensure that the sides have released from the dish. To plate the flan, place a plate over the top of the soufflé dish, and carefully flip it. Slide the flan from the small plate to a cake stand. The caramel sauce will be oozing over the top of the flan. Sprinkle with shredded coconut, slice, and serve.

Serves 8

urban escape

For the first eighteen years of our lives, Hayley and I lived in the suburbs of Pittsburgh. For those of you who are not familiar with this city, it is one of contrast. What was once a notoriously dirty center of industry (steel, namely) is now one of the up and coming cities in America for environmental sustainability. We have the world's largest green building, the most bridges (446), and three beautiful rivers that wind their way through rolling green hills. It's a pretty great place to live, and we are proud to call it home.

In my college years, I was given the opportunity to study abroad in Rome. My morning stroll to class started out down Via Garibaldi in Trastevere to get some breakfast—usually a pastry and a cappuccino. Those Italians take their coffee very seriously. I quickly learned the way of the working class there: Order quickly and drink even quicker. I spent my days painting, learning about ancient cities, and taking photos.

Then, after college, I moved to Northern Virginia for my first "real" job with a landscape architecture firm in Old Town Alexandria. That is where the entertaining bug bit. I lived in a townhouse with a few coworkers, and we all enjoyed throwing parties. The ambiance fell somewhere between college frat party and sophisticated gourmet dinner, but the love of bringing friends together and cooking for them was something that really stuck with me.

The company and the setting for this meal were both clear choices. My sister, Nellie, and her husband, Chris, had just moved back to Pittsburgh in early 2012 after several years in Boston. Their new apartment is in the Cultural District of Pittsburgh, and the building's rooftop terrace is only steps away from their door. Along with my parents, Hayley and I welcomed Nellie and Chris back to Pittsburgh in style with a memorable evening on their rooftop terrace.

This meal is both a celebration of city life and a bit of a refuge from it, too. Good food can be an escape from the rushed pace of life, and that's what we sought to do when we designed this menu. You don't necessarily need an elaborate rooftop set-up for this dinner (or a city for that matter). The urban theme is carried to the table with square place settings that echo the architectural lines of the skyscrapers in the background. Cool hues in the table settings also play off of the colors of steel and glass.

menu

Crab-Stuffed Artichoke Bottoms

Spiced Nuts with Rosemary and Thyme

Pan-Seared Lamb Chops with Rhubarb Chutney

Sautéed Japanese Eggplant and Onions with Sage

Blackberry Cobbler with Vanilla Bean Ice Cream

Shopping and Preparation

Entertaining guests in an apartment can be intimidating. With a small amount of working space and not as many options for types of cooking, you may feel as though it can't be done. Keeping the dishes simple with quick cooking methods like pan-searing and sautéing are the best way to execute a flawless dinner in an urban kitchen.

For this meal, you can keep table decor to a minimum because the beauty of the city and lights all around you will be more than enough to delight your guests.

Three days ahead

Make the ice cream, aioli, and spiced nuts. Keep the nuts in the refrigerator until just before your guests arrive.

One day ahead

Head to the market to grab any last-minute items, and the fresh meat, flowers, and produce. Items to be cooked on this day are the chutney, the crab stuffing, and the cobbler.

The day of the dinner

Thirty minutes before guests arrive, sauté the eggplant, and leave it on the stove to keep warm until serving.

As your guests arrive

Set out the appetizers, water pitchers, and the wine. If there are any leftover blackberries, set those out for guests to munch on as well. After mingling and grabbing a bite of food, you can steal away to the kitchen to pan-sear the main course and finish the dinner for serving.

Thirty minutes after your guests arrive

Start preparing the dinner. Warm the chutney, sauté the eggplant and onions, and sear the lamb chops. Plate the dinner, and allow it to sit while you remove the appetizer plates, and set the table with flatware.

Be sure to refresh your guests' wine glasses. Then, set out the dinner, and allow guests to serve themselves. Before sitting down, remove the cobbler from the refrigerator, and allow it to come to room temperature.

Once dinner has come to an end, place the cobbler back in the oven to warm. Then, uncover it, and broil it for 5 minutes until the top is golden brown and toasted.

Clear the dinner plates, and bring out the dessert plates. If you really want to impress your guests, torch the top of the cobbler at the table instead of broiling it. Serve the cobbler topped with a scoop of vanilla ice cream. Sit back, and enjoy the rest of your evening.

crab-stuffed artichoke bottoms

This light and fresh appetizer sets an elegant tone at the start of the meal. You can prepare the crab stuffing up to a day in advance, making this dish simple to put together the day of the party.

To make the macadamia nut aioli, blend the egg, lemon juice, and mustard seed in a blender or food processor. Slowly add in the macadamia nut oil, one tablespoon at a time, continuing to blend. When the oil has all emulsified and you have a creamy mayonnaise, add the salt and pepper, and continue to blend until desired consistency.

Scoop the lump crab meat into a medium-sized mixing bowl. Stir a half cup of the aioli into the crab meat. Add the garlic powder, onion powder, salt, and black pepper, and stir to combine. Add the fresh dill and chives, and mix until all ingredients are thoroughly combined. Crab stuffing is best prepared a day in advance so that all of the flavors can marinate for 24 hours.

Drain the artichoke bottoms from the brine, and place them in a water bath for 1 hour to remove the brine. Dry the artichokes with a paper towel, and place them on a large platter. Using a small ice cream scoop, place the crab stuffing into the artichoke bottoms. Garnish each with fresh chives, and refrigerate until serving time.

Serves 6

1/2 cup macadamia nut aioli

   1 pastured egg

   1 tablespoon lemon juice

   1/4 teaspoon yellow mustard seed, ground

   1 cup macadamia nut oil

   1/2 teaspoon salt

   1/2 teaspoon black pepper

1 pound wild-caught lump crab meat

1 teaspoon garlic powder

1 teaspoon onion powder

1/2 teaspoon salt

1 teaspoon black pepper

2 tablespoons fresh dill, minced

2 tablespoons fresh chives, minced

3 cans artichoke bottoms (18 bottoms)

1 cup raw almonds

1 cup raw walnuts

1 cup raw pecans

3 tablespoons unsalted grass-fed butter

2 tablespoons maple sugar

1/2 teaspoon ground cinnamon

2 tablespoons fresh rosemary, minced

2 tablespoons fresh thyme, minced

1 teaspoon salt

spiced nuts with rosemary and thyme

As guests get settled in with drinks and conversation, this dish becomes a key player. Keep these spiced nuts within arm's reach by placing a few small dishes of them out for guests to munch on as they chat.

Preheat your oven to 300 degrees. Place the raw almonds, walnuts, and pecans on a large, parchment-lined baking sheet.

In a medium-sized saucepan, warm the butter over medium-low heat. Once the butter has melted, add the maple sugar, cinnamon, rosemary, and thyme. Stir continuously until the herbs have started to soften. Pour the mixture over the nuts, and stir to coat evenly. Sprinkle the nuts with salt.

Place the nuts in the oven for 10 minutes. Then, stir them, and place them in the oven for another 10 minutes. Check the nuts again, and if they are not toasted enough, bake them for an additional 2 minutes. Allow the nuts to cool, and keep them refrigerated up to 1 week until use.

Serves 6

Rhubarb Chutney

1 tablespoon grass-fed butter

1 small red onion, finely diced

2 cloves garlic, minced

1/2 teaspoon allspice

1/2 teaspoon salt

1 tablespoon ginger root, grated

2 stalks rhubarb, sliced into 1/4-inch pieces

1/3 cup water

1 tablespoon white balsamic vinegar

10 medjool dates, pitted and chopped

1/4 cup maple syrup

Lamb Chops

4 tablespoons grass-fed butter
   (separated into two portions)

2 racks of lamb, cut into chops

Salt and pepper to taste

pan-seared lamb chops with rhubarb chutney

Pan-seared lamb chops are an excellent choice of main dish for city dwellers who like to entertain. A quick sear in the pan, followed by a pop in the oven, is all you need to create exquisite medium-rare chops.

In a large saucepan, melt 1 tablespoon of the butter over medium-low heat. Add the onion, garlic, allspice, salt, and ginger to the pan, and sauté until the onion and garlic are translucent. Add the rhubarb, water, vinegar, and dates to the pot, and stir to combine all ingredients. Add the maple syrup, stir again, and bring the mixture to a low boil. Cook the chutney until the dates and rhubarb are soft. This recipe can be made 1-2 days in advance and kept chilled in the refrigerator. Warm in a saucepan just prior to use.

To cook the lamb chops, preheat your oven to 400 degrees. Heat an oven-safe skillet over medium heat, adding a tablespoon of butter. If you have two oven-safe skillets, prepare both similarly as it will make cooking the lamb chops quicker and easier. Sear the lamb chops 2 minutes on a side. Then, place them in the oven for 2 more minutes. When one set of chops is finished, add salt and pepper to taste, plate them, and add more butter as needed before searing the additional lamb chops.

Serves 6

sautéed japanese eggplant with onions and sage

This dish comes together quickly, which is a necessity when you're entertaining guests. The wonderful aroma of the vegetables sautéing in the butter will fill your home and greet your guests when they arrive.

Heat a large skillet over medium heat. Add one tablespoon of butter to coat the skillet. Add the eggplant, onion, and sage to the skillet, and sauté. Add salt and pepper, as well as additional butter if needed. Sauté until the onions are soft and translucent and the eggplant is seared on both sides and soft in the middle (about 30 minutes).

Serves 6

2 tablespoons grass-fed butter

12 Japanese eggplants, chopped into
1/2-inch slices

1 yellow onion, thinly sliced

1 bunch fresh sage, chopped

Salt and pepper to taste

blackberry cobbler with vanilla bean ice cream

As your guests start eating dinner, slip into the kitchen and place the cobbler back in the oven to warm. When the time comes for dessert, bring the cobbler out, and toast the crust with a kitchen torch. Top the hot cobbler with a scoop of vanilla bean ice cream. Delicious!

Vanilla Bean Ice Cream
- 16 fluid ounces coconut milk, full fat
- 1/4 cup maple syrup
- 3 egg yolks
- 1 vanilla bean pod, seeds only

Blackberry Cobbler
- 1 1/2 cups blanched almond flour
- 1/2 teaspoon salt
- 1/2 teaspoon baking soda
- Zest of half a lemon
- 2 eggs
- 2 teaspoons pure vanilla extract
- 1/2 cup maple syrup
- 2 tablespoons grass-fed butter, melted
- 12 ounces fresh blackberries

In a medium-sized saucepan, combine the coconut milk, maple syrup, and egg yolks. Bring the mixture to a low boil while whisking. Then, let it cool. When the mixture is cool, strain it into a medium mixing bowl. Add the seeds from the vanilla bean, stir, and cover the bowl with plastic wrap. Chill the mixture in the refrigerator for 2 hours. Place the mixture in an ice cream maker, and process it until the desired consistency is reached.

To make the cobbler, preheat your oven to 350 degrees. In a medium-sized mixing bowl, combine the almond flour, salt, baking soda, and lemon zest.

In a separate small mixing bowl, add the eggs, vanilla extract, maple syrup, and butter. Blend the mixture with a hand mixer until smooth. Add the wet mixture to the dry mixture, and blend together with a hand mixer until smooth.

Fold the blackberries into the batter, and pour the batter into a lightly greased, 9-inch baking dish. Cover the baking dish, and bake for 50 minutes.

Remove the cobbler from the oven, and allow it to cool, refrigerating if necessary. Before serving, warm the cobbler at 300 degrees for 20 minutes. Remove it from the oven, and brown the crust with a kitchen torch (at the table) or by broiling. If broiling, remove the lid, and turn the oven temperature to broil at 500 degrees. Place the oven rack on the very top setting, and broil the cobbler for 5 minutes or until the top has formed a golden brown toasted crust. Cut and immediately serve with ice cream.

Serves 8

harvest dinner

Supporting your local farmer is very rewarding. You know you're consuming an animal that lived a wonderful life and was happy, healthy, and treated humanely. Plus, your hard-earned dollars are spent on a product that someone worked extremely hard to supply. Farming is tough work that takes truly devoted people. This is especially true when that farmer does the work with integrity by raising their animals as they should be raised—on pasture with room to roam and eating the appropriate foods.

When you're new to sourcing your food locally, it can be a daunting task trying to figure out where you can get meat and produce other than the grocery store. This year, we learned that we live very close to a farmer raising his animals as they should be raised. This particular farmer is a good friend of my (Hayley's) aunt and uncle, and he's raising animals on his own land. He has a passion for farming and spends all of his free time tending to his happy and healthy animals. Then, at the end of the day, he conducts research to learn how he can make his farming practices even better for the next season. We truly enjoyed getting to know our farmer friend this past year and have taken every opportunity to patronize his new farming operation.

So, for this menu, we were able to go through our farmer's personal freezer and pick out the cuts of meat we wanted to highlight for the dinner. We showed our gratitude by serving this meal to him and his family. We used our creativity to make dishes that would complement the cuts of meat, and they turned out great! We were so grateful that we had the opportunity to source the food locally for this meal and feed the farmer who works so hard to provide these honest products.

menu

Cherry and Walnut Salad
with Fig Balsamic Vinaigrette

Pumpkin Chicken Chili

Apple-Glazed Pork Loin

Honeycrisp Applesauce

Baked Acorn Squash

Pumpkin Torte with Cream Cheese
Frosting and Caramel

Shopping and Preparation

Fall is the flavor of this menu. Autumn colors fill the table, and small accents of acorns show your guests that you really went above and beyond to make the evening special and festive. Autumn leaves, gourds, and Indian corn are a beautiful way to style your table and can be found at many markets in the fall for a reasonable price. We found napkin holders in the shape of leaves, for example. Another option would be to wrap the napkin with a tree leaf, and tie it with butcher's twine. A centerpiece of fresh fall flowers will complete this table setting.

Two days ahead

Today, remove any frozen meats from the freezer to defrost in the refrigerator. At this time, you can also make the fresh apple sauce and gather any last-minute produce items.

One day before

Set and decorate the table, and purchase your flower centerpiece. The pumpkin chili is a dish that can be made a day ahead of time. This will keep the stress of cooking the meal low tomorrow. You can also make the torte today, but leave frosting for tomorrow.

One hour before dinner

At this point, you can prep the acorn squash for baking. This is also the time to make the salad, but dress the salad just before serving. Be sure that your guests are comfortable as they arrive and that they have a drink in hand.

cherry and walnut salad with fig balsamic vinaigrette

This salad brings much needed lightness to an otherwise rich and hearty meal. The sweet flavors of fig really pop through the balsamic dressing, and give a unique taste to the dish.

In a large bowl, place approximately 8 cups of the mixed salad greens. Toss the red onion with the greens, and add the dried cherries and walnuts.

In a separate small mixing bowl, whisk together the olive oil and the balsamic vinegar. Sprinkle the salad with salt and pepper to taste, and serve tossed.

Serves 12

8 cups mixed salad greens
1/4 cup red onion, chopped
1 cup dried cherries
1 cup walnuts
1/8 cup extra-virgin olive oil
1/4 cup fig balsamic vinegar*
Salt and pepper to taste

*If you cannot find fig balsamic vinegar, any balsamic vinegar will work. (We also like cherry balsamic).

*Pumpkin Chili Spice

   1 tablespoon onion powder

   1 tablespoon garlic powder

   1 tablespoon chipotle powder

   1 1/2 tablespoons ground cinnamon

   1/2 tablespoon smoked paprika

   1 teaspoon ground nutmeg

   1/2 teaspoon ground ginger

Chili

   2-3 tablespoons duck fat

   7 pounds chicken, skin removed and cubed

   1 large yellow onion, roughly chopped

   2 tablespoons pumpkin chili spice* (see above)

   3 green bell peppers, seeded and

      cut into bite-sized pieces

   28 ounces fire-roasted tomatoes

      (about 2 cans)

   6 ounces tomato paste

   2 cups chicken stock

   14 ounces puréed pumpkin

   Salt and pepper to taste

pumpkin chicken chili

Pumpkin is a great way to bring harvest flavors to a classic chili dish. We used a whole pasture-raised chicken for this recipe, but you could also use beef or pork in its place.

In a small bowl, combine the onion powder, garlic powder, chipotle powder, cinnamon, smoked paprika, nutmeg, and ginger to make the Pumpkin Chili Spice. Set aside.

Heat a large skillet over medium-high heat. Add 1 tablespoon of duck fat to the skillet, and add half of the chicken to the skillet, along with half of the onion. Season with half a tablespoon of Pumpkin Chili Spice, and brown the chicken on all sides. Transfer the chicken and onions to a large Dutch oven. Repeat the process in the skillet with the second batch of chicken, onion, and spice.

Heat the Dutch oven over medium heat, and add the green bell peppers, chicken stock, fire-roasted tomatoes, tomato paste, and puréed pumpkin. Stir until all ingredients are combined. Season with 1 tablespoon of pumpkin chili spice, salt, and black pepper.

Bring the chili to a boil, turn it down to low, and cook for 4 hours. The chili can simmer on the stove until time to serve.

Serves 12

apple-glazed pork loin

This apple-glazed pork loin is an elegant way to present the classic flavor pairing of pork chops and applesauce. The sweet honeycrisp applesauce layered over the balsamic glaze packs big flavor into this dish.

To make the marinade, in a small bowl, whisk together the mustard and vinegar until smooth. Refrigerate until ready to use.

Preheat your oven to 350 degrees. Place the pork loin in a large baking dish, fat side up. Sprinkle the pork generously with salt and black pepper. Baste with mustard marinade. Bake pork loin 25 minutes per pound at 350 degrees.

After 45 minutes, baste the pork with the marinade, and pour 2 cups of applesauce over it. If it starts to burn, tent the pork with foil. Continue to bake until the pork reaches 170 degrees internally on a meat thermometer. Slice, and serve the pork loin with the applesauce.

Serves 12

Mustard Marinade/Glaze

    2 tablespoons spicy brown mustard

    *1/2 cup fig balsamic vinegar

Pork Loin

    5 pounds pork loin

    Salt and pepper to taste

    Mustard Marinade (above)

    2 cups Honeycrisp Applesauce (pg 192)

*If you cannot find fig balsamic vinegar, any balsamic vinegar will work.

4 honeycrisp apples, cored
1 teaspoon ground cinnamon
1/2 teaspoon ground nutmeg
1 cinnamon stick

honeycrisp applesauce

Apple season is a favorite time of ours here in Pennsylvania. One of our best-loved varieties is honeycrisp, which we like to make into a sweet applesauce. This is a great side dish that goes well with most roasted meats.

Cut the apples into large chunks, discarding the cores. Place the apple pieces into a food processor or high-speed blender. Add the cinnamon and nutmeg, and pulse the apples until they are mostly smooth, but still slightly chunky.

Place the pureed apples, along with a cinnamon stick into a slow cooker, and cook on high for 1 hour. Stir the apples, set the temperature to low, and cook for another hour. Remove the cinnamon stick, and serve the applesauce warm.

Serves 12

baked acorn squash

Fall is the best time of year to enjoy fresh winter squash, which is coming into season in most locales. The warm flavors and aromas of cinnamon and nutmeg perfectly complement this dish, while the crunch of the chopped walnuts adds a pleasant layer of texture.

Preheat your oven to 350 degrees. Remove the stem ends of the squash, and cut it in half. Scoop out the seeds, and place a half tablespoon of butter into each half of the squash. Sprinkle the squash with cinnamon, nutmeg, salt, and pepper.

Bake the squash until it is fork tender, about 45 minutes. After roasting, cut it in half again before serving. Garnish it with the chopped walnuts.

Serves 12

3 whole acorn squash, cut in half
   and seeds removed
4 tablespoons grass-fed butter
Pinch of cinnamon for each squash half
Pinch of nutmeg for each squash half
Salt and pepper to taste
1/2 cup chopped walnuts

pumpkin torte with cream cheese frosting and caramel

Enjoy fall flavors in a new way with this layered pumpkin torte. Whipped cream cheese frosting adds a refreshing flavor and lightness to an otherwise rich and dense cake.

3/4 cup coconut flour, sifted
1 teaspoon sea salt
2 teaspoons cinnamon
1 teaspoon baking soda
10 eggs
1 tablespoon pure vanilla extract
1 cup pure maple syrup
1 cup coconut oil, melted
8 ounces pumpkin purée (1/2 can)

Frosting and Topping
    16 ounces cream cheese, softened
    1/4 cup pure maple syrup
    1/2 cup pecans, chopped

Preheat your oven to 325 degrees. In a small bowl, add the sifted coconut flour, salt, cinnamon, and baking soda.

In a separate large bowl or kitchen mixer, combine the eggs, vanilla extract, maple syrup, melted coconut oil, and pumpkin purée. Add the dry ingredients to the wet ingredients, and continue to blend them with the mixer until the batter is smooth.

Grease two 9-inch cake pans with coconut oil. Pour the batter into the pans, taking care to split it equally.

Bake the cakes for 35 minutes. Test the center of the cakes with a toothpick. If the toothpick comes out clean, they are done. Remove the cakes from the oven, and allow them to cool.

While the cakes are cooling, use a standing mixer or a bowl and hand mixer to blend together the cream cheese and maple syrup for the frosting until evenly mixed. Frost the cool cakes, and sprinkle them with the chopped pecans.

Serves 12

spooky supper

Halloween is always an exciting holiday! You get to dress up in costume with your friends, eat tasty treats, and even take part in some scary activities.

We had a lot of fun creating this menu for Halloween. So many of the food items that we try to eat on a regular basis seem scary or strange to others. Beef heart is only something a witch would eat, not a normal person, right? Organ meats (also known as "offal") are important foods to incorporate into a well-balanced human diet. Creating interesting dishes for Halloween using these meats has been a fun way to do just that.

Along with heart, bone marrow, and "eyeballs," we also enjoyed making fun desserts because we all know that the best part of

Halloween is going trick or treating for candy. We feel it's important for everyone to get to enjoy holiday traditions, even when following a healthy diet. For us, this means celebrating with fun, grain-free desserts that use natural sugars.

Spooky cutout cookies made with almond flour and fluffy chocolate cupcakes made with coconut flour will allow you to enjoy this tasty holiday and still feel good about what you put into your body.

This Halloween, dress up, and have a blast with your friends, knowing that you will be nourishing your body while you do it.

menu

· · · · · · · · · · · · · · · · · · · ·

Roasted Marrow Bones

Ghostly Pear Guacamole with Fried Plantain Chips

Beef Heart Stew

Spaghetti and "Eyeballs"

"Bleeding" Cupcakes

Mummy Cookies or Black and White Bones

Caramel Crab Apples

Shopping and Preparation

You can find fun and spooky decorations for your Halloween dinner table at any party store. Dress the chairs with fake cobwebs, and scatter the table with plastic spiders.

A cauldron roiling with fog makes a fantastically fun centerpiece. Fill the cauldron 3/4-full with warm tap water, and drop in a sizeable piece of dry ice. A fist-sized chunk will make fog for about 15 minutes.

Five days before the party

Shop for your table decorations, and get your Halloween costumes.

One day before the party

This is the day to do the remainder of the food shopping. Pick up any remaining produce, fresh marrow bones for roasting, and the dry ice for the table. Make the stew, and bake the cookies and the cupcakes. You can also frost the desserts and keep them in the refrigerator overnight.

The day of the party

Finish up any remaining Halloween decorations and get the table ready for serving. A few hours before the party, warm the stew on the stove. Plate the desserts, and have them on display. They will double as decorations and treats!

As your guests arrive

Light the candles on your table, and fill your cauldron with dry ice and water. Your guests will "ooh" and "ahhh" as they walk through your door.

roasted marrow bones

Preheat your oven to 425 degrees. Place the marrow bones in a baking dish, and bake them until the marrow is soft (aboug 20-25 minutes). Sprinkle them with salt, and garnish with parsley.

Serves 10

Roasted Marrow Bones
   5 marrow bones, cut in half lengthwise
   Sea salt
   Fresh parsley for garnish

Pear Guacamole
   5 Haas avocados
   2 teaspoons onion powder
   2 teaspoons garlic powder
   1 Asian pear, diced
   1/4 cup cilantro, diced
   Juice of 1 lime
   Salt and pepper to taste

Plantain Chips
   1 cup coconut oil
   5 green plantains, thinly sliced
   Spice mixture
      1 tablespoon smoked paprika
      1/2 tablespoon onion powder
      1 teaspoon cinnamon
      1 teaspoon coriander
      1 teaspoon salt
      1 teaspoon black pepper

ghostly pear guacamole with fried plantain chips

In a medium-sized mixing bowl, mash the avocados with a fork. Add the onion powder and garlic powder, and stir to combine. Add the diced pear, cilantro, lime juice, salt, and pepper. Stir to evenly combine all ingredients.

In a small mixing bowl, stir together the spice mixture of smoked paprika, onion powder, cinnamon, coriander, salt, and black pepper.

To make the plantain chips, heat the coconut oil in a large Dutch oven. Add 1 thinly sliced plantain to the pot, and fry it until golden brown. Remove it from the pot, and drain the oils on a towel. Season the fried plantains with the spice mixture, and repeat with the remaining plantains. Serve alongside guacamole.

Serves 10

beef heart stew

Considered by many to be a superfood, beef heart is the perfect addition to a warm bowl of soup or stew. Heart is a muscle, so this particular organ will have a texture more similar to that of steak. This affordable cut of protein is packed full of B vitamins, folate, and zinc. Not only will you have a festive dish to serve your guests, but you will be offering an item full of important nutrients to go with it!

2 tablespoons beef tallow (beef fat)*

3 pounds London broil, cut into bite-sized pieces

1 pound beef heart, cut into bite-sized pieces

4 large carrots, cut into bite-sized pieces

1 large onion, cut into bite-sized pieces

Sea salt to taste

1 cup of red wine

2-4 cups of beef stock (just enough to
    cover the meat)

3 tablespoons arrowroot flour

Heat a skillet over medium heat. Add the beef tallow to the skillet and warm it. Add the meat to the skillet in three batches, and sear on all sides. Then, place it into a large Dutch oven. When all of the meat has been browned, sauté the carrots and onion in the skillet.

When the carrots have browned slightly and the onions have softened, add them to the Dutch oven. Sprinkle everything with sea salt, and pour one cup of red wine over the mixture.

Turn the burner to medium heat, and add enough beef stock so that the liquid is just covering the meat. Cover, and bring to a boil. Then, turn down the heat to simmer and cook for 4 hours. When there are 20 minutes left of cooking, add the arrowroot flour and stir to thicken the sauce slightly.

Serves 10

*You can use another high quality cooking fat in place of the tallow, such as lard, coconut oil, or grass-fed butter.

spaghetti and "eyeballs"

You are bound to get the kiddos gasping and giggling when you put a plate of what looks to be eyeballs in front of them. This is a simple recipe that is tons of fun to serve on Halloween, and the kids can help! They will love to "smush" the olive into the meatball for baking, and no matter what they look like, these "eyeballs" couldn't be tastier.

Heat a medium-sized saucepan over medium heat. Add the duck fat and onion to the pan, and sauté the onion until translucent. Add the tomato sauce, tomato paste, and balsamic vinegar. Stir to combine all ingredients. Season with oregano, salt, and pepper. Allow the sauce to come to a low boil, turn down to a simmer, and cover. Simmer the sauce until time for serving.

Preheat your oven to 350 degrees. Slice the spaghetti squash in half, and remove the seeds. Place the spaghetti squash in a baking dish, and bake for 35 minutes or until fork-tender.

In a large mixing bowl, combine the ground beef, garlic, shallot, salt, and pepper. Roll the meat into 1-ounce meatballs, and place them on a baking sheet. Stuff each green olive with a pimento, and place 1 olive in the center of each meatball to create an "eye." Bake the meatballs for 30 minutes.

Remove the squash from the oven, allow it to cool enough to touch, and shred the squash with a fork to create "noodles." Plate the spaghetti squash in a large bowl. Top it with the sauce, but do not toss. Top the squash and sauce with several meat "eyeballs." After presenting the dish, toss it to evenly coat the squash with sauce.

Serves 10

Sauce

1 tablespoon duck fat

1 small onion, diced

2 15-ounce cans tomato sauce
(no salt added)

1 6-ounce can tomato paste

1/4 cup balsamic vinegar

2 tablespoons dried oregano

Salt and pepper to taste

Spaghetti

2 large spaghetti squash

"Eyeballs"

3 pounds ground beef

3 cloves minced garlic

1 minced shallot

Salt and pepper to taste

24 green olives, one for each meatball

1 small jar of pimentos

"bleeding" cupcakes

Bright red "goo" in the center of a dark chocolate cupcake is a delicious way to surprise your guests. These tasty little cakes are covered in dark black oozing chocolate frosting, which will have you licking every finger clean.

Preheat your oven to 350 degrees. In a small mixing bowl, blend the eggs, maple syrup, coconut milk, palm shortening, and vanilla extract with a hand mixer.

In a separate large mixing bowl, combine the coconut flour, salt, baking powder, and cocoa powder. Pour the wet ingredients into the dry ingredients, and blend with a hand mixer until the batter is smooth. Pour the batter into a lined cupcake pan, and bake for 35 minutes.

Allow the cupcakes to cool. Then, remove the center of each cupcake with an apple corer or a cupcake plunger. Save the tops of the cupcakes for sealing the filling before frosting.

Warm a medium-sized saucepan over medium heat. Add 1 cup raspberries, 1/4 cup of water, maple syrup, and lemon juice to the pan. Stir all ingredients, and bring the liquid to a low boil. Whisk the arrowroot into the mixture, and continue to boil until the arrowroot has fully dissolved and the filling starts to thicken. Once the filling has a jelly-like consistency, remove the pan from the burner, and allow the liquid to cool. Stir in the remaining raspberries, and fill each cupcake with enough of the raspberry filling to reach the top of the cupcake. Seal each with the tops.

In a small saucepan, heat the cream and butter over medium heat. Bring the cream and butter mixture to a boil while swirling them around to combine the ingredients. Pour the chocolate chips into a medium-sized bowl. Pour the cream and butter over the chocolate chips, and stir until the chocolate melts and the sauce thickens. Allow the mixture to cool, and pour it over the cupcakes. Serve immediately, or refrigerate the cupcakes before serving to harden the frosting slightly.

Serves 10

Cupcakes

6 eggs

1/2 cup pure maple syrup

1/4 cup coconut milk

1/2 cup palm shortening, melted

1 teaspoon pure vanilla extract

1/2 cup coconut flour, sifted

1 teaspoon salt

3/4 teaspoon gluten-free baking powder

1/4 cup cocoa powder

Raspberry Filling

2 cups frozen raspberries, thawed

1/4 cup water

3 tablespoons pure maple syrup

1 teaspoon lemon juice

2 tablespoons arrowroot flour

Oozing Dark Chocolate Icing

3/4 cup heavy whipping cream

1 tablespoon grass-fed butter

1 cup dark chocolate chips

mummy cookies
black and white bones

These cookies may look different, but they share the same basic dough. These two variations on a grain-free sugar cookie are easy to make and can be a fun project for your little ones to decorate. Get creative with different cookie cutters and decorations for more variety.

1 egg

1/2 cup pure maple syrup

2 tablespoons palm shortening, melted

3 cups blanched almond flour

1/2 cup arrowroot flour + more for dusting

1/2 teaspoon salt

1 teaspoon gluten-free baking powder

Garnish

    1/4 cup currants

    Oozing Dark Chocolate Icing (pg 210)

    Coconut Cream Frosting (below)

Coconut Cream Frosting

    1/2 cup coconut butter

    2 tablespoons coconut oil

    1 tablespoon pure maple syrup

Preheat your oven to 325 degrees. In a small mixing bowl, combine the egg, maple syrup, and palm shortening. Blend the ingredients with a hand mixer until smooth.

In a separate large mixing bowl, combine the almond flour, arrowroot flour, salt, and baking powder. Pour the wet ingredients into the dry ingredients, and blend with the mixer until it forms a smooth dough.

Line a baking sheet with parchment paper, and dust the paper with a good amount of arrowroot flour. Place the ball of cookie dough on the baking sheet, and dust the top of the dough with more arrowroot flour. Place another piece of parchment paper on top of the dough, and roll it out to 1/4-inch thickness. Dust the dough with more arrowroot flour, and dust the cookie cutters with arrowroot flour as well. (It's helpful to pour arrowroot flour onto a small dish and dip the cookie cutter into the dish for dusting.)

Cut out gingerbread men shapes and bone-shape cookies. Carefully remove the leftover dough from around the cookie cutters, and place the cookies on a baking sheet by just moving the parchment paper they are already on. Repeat the cookie cutting steps with the remaining dough until you have the amount of cookies you would like or until there is no dough left. Before baking, place two currants into each of the gingerbread men cookies to make mummy eyes. Bake the cookies for 15 minutes, and allow them to cool before frosting them.

To make the coconut cream frosting, warm the coconut butter over medium-low heat in a small saucepan, add the coconut oil and maple syrup to the saucepan, and stir to combine. Heat until soft but not fully liquid. Pour the frosting into a heat-safe piping bag, and using a small-tipped piping applicator, dress the cookies with "ribbons" of frosting. For the black and white bones, dip half of the bones into the Oozing Dark Chocolate Icing (see page 210), and refrigerate them to set the icing.

Serves 10

caramel crab apples

Caramel apples are a favorite sweet treat among children (and adults) during the fall season. We made our own little candy apples using an heirloom variety called lady apples, which are about the size of a clementine tangerine. These bite-sized caramel apples are a cute and fun treat that you can make ahead of time for your party.

In a small saucepan, combine the heavy cream, butter, and salt together over medium-high heat. Allow the cream to come to a boil. Then, reduce the heat, and set the pan aside.

In a separate medium saucepan, add the maple sugar, maple syrup, and water. Stir the ingredients until they are dissolved as you heat them over medium-high heat. When the mixture starts to bubble, add the heavy cream mixture from the small saucepan. Turn up the heat slightly, stirring frequently. When the caramel reaches 250 degrees Fahrenheit, remove it from the heat, and allow it to cool for approximately 5 minutes.

Remove the stems from the apples using a sharp paring knife. Carefully push a candy stick down through the core of each apple, making sure the sticks are firmly in place but do not go through the apple. Dip the apples in the caramel so that they are evenly covered, and immediately sprinkle them with dark chocolate chips.

Allow the caramel apples to cool on parchment paper or wax paper. Refrigerate them until serving.

Serves 10

1 cup heavy cream
5 tablespoons grass-fed butter
1 teaspoon salt
1 1/2 cups maple sugar
1/4 cup maple syrup
1/4 cup water
10 lady apples
1/2 cup dark chocolate chips

Candy sticks
Candy thermometer

thanksgiving feast

Thanksgiving has always been a special holiday to me (Hayley). Growing up, we often celebrated Thanksgiving with my dad's parents in Ohio. My Grandma Jo is an amazing cook, and I have always loved her meals.

My mom's mother is also a fantastic cook, and she always took the time to teach me about cooking. But, it was actually my Grandy Kyp who was the first person I remember teaching me how to cook Thanksgiving dishes.

Thanksgiving is the perfect holiday to share the cooking chores with family. I have had family dinners that were prepared by one person, but the most enjoyable ones are those that involve the whole family. I have fond memories of my mom, aunts, and Grandy stuffing the bird and making the gravy, all while my uncle set the table.

The first holiday I spent with Bill's family was Thanksgiving. We got to cook with his mom, Nellie. From the beginning of our relationship, I knew we would be making new memories of Thanksgiving dinners together.

This Thanksgiving was spent with my family. Bill and I were given the reins to make a grain-free feast for all to enjoy. This was the year that we started making new traditions. There were a few classic dishes that my mom and aunts still made, but the family loved to taste the new dishes that Bill and I created.

We are thankful to have a happy and healthy family to share in these holiday traditions, both new and old.

menu

· ·

Cranberry Relish

Poached Pear Salad

Lemon Green Beans with Shallots

Apple Veal Stuffing

Stuffed Turkey Rubbed with Duck Fat
and Herbs

Pecan Pie

Shopping and Preparation

Five days ahead

Prepare the table settings. Colorful fall leaves, pumpkins, gourds, and colorful Indian corn are festive and inexpensive table decorations. Several different heights of candles also add warmth to this meal of comfort food.

Three days ahead

If your turkey is frozen, begin to defrost it in the refrigerator at least three days in advance. A large turkey can take several days to defrost. Today is also the day to do most of your grocery shopping. All produce should be purchased today, as well as the ground meat for the stuffing.

One day ahead

Make the pie and cranberry relish. Poach the pears, and pre-make the stuffing without adding the apples. Also, roast the nuts for the salad. Set and decorate the table today so that it's ready for the big dinner tomorrow.

Five hours before dinner

Prepare the turkey for stuffing and roasting. At this point, you can get a pot of water simmering with the giblets, neck, celery, and onion for basting.

One hour before the party

Put the green beans in to roast, put together the salad, and make sure all of the food items are in their serving dishes. The turkey will be coming out of the oven soon and will need to rest 30-60 minutes before being carved.

As dinner comes to an end

Remove the pie from the refrigerator, and allow it to come to room temperature. Brew coffee for you guests, and whip some cream to serve with the pie.

3 pounds fresh cranberries

3 cups water + 3 tablespoons

3 cups medjool dates, pitted and packed

cranberry relish

Due to their sometimes bitter flavor, cranberries elicit a love or hate response from most people. When we make Thanksgiving dinner, we add a generous helping of smashed medjool dates to take the tart edge off of the cranberries. This recipe is sure to evoke a "love 'em" response, so plan to make extra servings!

In a large saucepan, add the cranberries and 3 cups of water. Turn the burner to medium heat, and cook the cranberries until they pop.

While the cranberries are cooking, in a medium-sized mixing bowl, add the dates and 3 tablespoons of water. Microwave the dates 45 seconds, mash the dates with a fork, add them to the cranberries, and stir to combine. Turn the heat on the cranberries down to low, and simmer them for 10 minutes, stirring frequently.

Once the dates have infused the cranberries with sweetness, remove the cranberries from the heat, and allow them to cool. This dish can be prepared a day ahead of time and refrigerated overnight.

Serves 10

poached pear salad

Some experts say that salad has no place at Thanksgiving, but we disagree. This dish provides a nice, light counterpoint to the rich and hearty dishes, bringing balance to your meal.

Preheat your oven to 325 degrees. In a small mixing bowl, whisk the egg whites and maple syrup. On a baking sheet, toss the pecans with the egg white and maple syrup, and generously sprinkle the pecans with the cinnamon, nutmeg, and ginger. Bake the pecans for 20-25 minutes or until lightly toasted.

Peel the pears, and cut the bottoms straight across so that the pears can stand up. In a medium-sized saucepan, add the pears, and pour in the grape juice to fill it half way. Cover the pot, and turn the flame to low. Poach the pears in the grape juice until soft. A knife should be able to slide through them easily, but the pears should still hold their shape. Remove the pears from the saucepan, and allow them to cool. Cut them into 1/2-inch cubes, discarding the cores.

Next, in a small mixing bowl, whisk together the spicy mustard, olive oil, and white balsamic vinegar.

On a large serving platter, combine the mixed greens, poached pear cubes, spiced pecans, and Gorgonzola cheese. Toss the salad with the dressing before serving.

Serves 10

Spiced Pecans

    1/2 cup egg whites

    1/4 cup maple syrup

    2 cups raw pecan halves

    1 tablespoon cinnamon

    1 tablespoon nutmeg

    1 tablespoon ginger

Poached Pears

    4 bosc pears (firm)

    2-3 cups grape juice

Dressing

    1 tablespoon spicy mustard

    1/2 cup extra-virgin olive oil

    1/4 cup white balsamic vinegar

Salad

    10 cups mixed greens

    1/2 cup Gorgonzola cheese, crumbled

lemon green beans with shallots

Side dishes are critical to the success of a good Thanksgiving dinner. Sure, the turkey is the star of the show, but having a variety of good side dishes will make the feast exponentially better. This easy-to-make dish won't distract you from the task at hand, and you can even have someone make this who doesn't normally cook.

2 pounds green beans

2 tablespoons coconut oil, melted

Salt and pepper to taste

Zest of 1 lemon

3 shallots, sliced

4 cloves garlic, minced

Preheat your oven to 400 degrees. Remove the ends of the green beans, and rinse them under cold water. Spread the green beans out on a large baking sheet (or two, if necessary). Drizzle the melted coconut oil over the green beans, and toss them to coat.

Sprinkle the green beans with the salt, pepper, and lemon zest. Top the beans with the sliced shallots. Roast the green beans and shallots for 20 minutes.

Add the minced garlic, toss to evenly distribute the garlic, and roast for 10 more minutes.

Serves 10

apple veal stuffing

It wouldn't be Thanksgiving without a little stuffing, but what are you to do when the only stuffing options are bread-based? Fret not! This veal-based stuffing is "a meal unto itself" as described by my brother-in-law, Chris, and it's a very satisfying substitute for traditional stuffing.

In a large mixing bowl, mix the ground veal with the garlic powder, anise, onion powder, black pepper, fennel seeds, paprika, salt, and cayenne.

Heat a large cast iron skillet over medium-high heat, and brown the meat, leaving it slightly under-done. Remove the skillet from the heat, and set the meat aside. When the meat has cooled, place it in the large bowl.

Add the mushrooms, celery, and onion to the skillet, and cook them until they are tender. Transfer the vegetables from the skillet to the bowl. Add the cranberries, chestnuts, garlic, rosemary, thyme, and sage. Allow the mixture to cool, and refrigerate it overnight if necessary.

Peel, core, and chop the Granny Smith apples. Then, add them to the meat mixture. For outside stuffing, bake the dish uncovered for the last 30 minutes during the cooking of the turkey.

Serves 10

3 pounds ground veal

1 tablespoon garlic powder

1 tablespoon anise

1 tablespoon onion powder

1 tablespoon black pepper

1 tablespoon fennel seeds

1/2 tablespoon paprika

1/2 tablespoon salt

1 teaspoon cayenne

24 ounces white mushrooms, chopped

2 celery hearts, chopped

1 onion, chopped

8 ounces dried cranberries

6 1/2 ounces chopped and cooked chestnuts

4 cloves garlic, minced

1/4 cup rosemary, minced

1/4 cup thyme, minced

1/3 cup sage, minced

3 medium Granny Smith apples

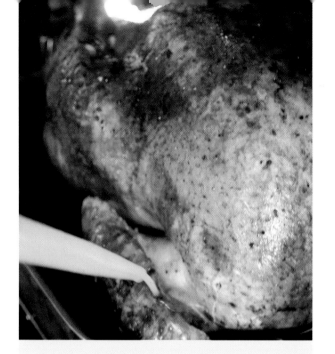

20-pound turkey (pasture-raised, if possible)

Compound
  3 tablespoons duck fat
  1 tablespoon rosemary, minced
  1 tablespoon thyme, minced
  Salt and pepper to taste

Stock for Basting
  1 onion
  3 large carrots
  5 stalks celery, plus the leafy heart
  Turkey neck and giblets
  2 cloves of garlic
  Salt and pepper to taste

stuffed turkey rubbed with duck fat and herbs

At the centerpiece of a traditional Thanksgiving table sits the turkey. Now, turkeys aren't naturally all that fatty. That's why we smother our turkey in duck fat, which also greatly enhances the flavor. Few dishes elicit the same salivary response as the wonderful aroma of a slowly roasting turkey in the oven.

Preheat your oven to 325 degrees. Rinse the turkey under cool water, and pat it dry, including the body cavity. Carefully lift the skin away from the meat.

In a small mixing bowl, combine the compound mixture using two tablespoons of duck fat, the rosemary, and the thyme. Rub the duck fat compound under the skin, covering as much of the breast and legs as possible.

Sprinkle the body cavity with salt and pepper. Rub the outer skin of the turkey with the remaining tablespoon of duck fat, and sprinkle it with salt and pepper. Stuff the bird cavity with the stuffing (see page 228), tie the legs with butcher's twine, and tuck the wings under the breast.

In a medium saucepan on the stove, place the onion, carrots, celery, turkey neck and giblets, garlic powder, salt, and pepper. Cover with water and boil. When the water has come to a boil, cover, and reduce the heat to low. Allow the stock to simmer while the turkey is cooking.

Place the turkey in a roasting pan filled with 1 inch of water. Roast the turkey at 325 degrees for 12 minutes per pound. Baste the turkey every 45 minutes with the stock. When the turkey is golden brown, cover it with a foil tent. The turkey will be finished when a meat thermometer reads 165 degrees in the thickest part of the breast.

Serves 10

Pie Crust

2 1/2 cups blanched almond flour

1/2 teaspoon salt

1/2 teaspoon baking soda

1/2 cup palm shortening, melted

2 tablespoons pure maple syrup

1 teaspoon pure vanilla extract

Filling

3 eggs

1/4 cup pure maple syrup

2 tablespoons molasses

1 teaspoon pure vanilla extract

1 cup date mixture

    6 medjool dates, pitted

    1/4 cup water

1/2 teaspoon salt

1 tablespoon coconut flour, sifted

1/4 cup grass-fed butter, melted

3/4 cup chopped pecans

1/2 cup pecan halves for garnish

pecan pie

Pecan pie is a tried and true Thanksgiving dessert. If you and your guests have saved any room for pie (which you should have), a slice will taste delicious with a cup of coffee.

Preheat your oven to 325 degrees. In a medium-sized bowl, combine the almond flour, salt, and baking soda.

In a separate small bowl, combine the melted palm shortening, maple syrup, and 1 teaspoon of vanilla extract. Stir the wet ingredients into the dry ingredients until it reaches a dough-y consistency. Pat the dough into a 9-inch glass pie dish, and bake for 10-15 minutes or until golden. Remove the crust from the oven to cool. Keep the oven set at 325 degrees.

In a standing mixer, combine the eggs, maple syrup, molasses, and 1 teaspoon of vanilla extract.

Place the dates and 1/4 cup of water in a medium-sized mixing bowl. Microwave the dates 45 seconds, mash the dates with a fork. Add the date mixture to the standing mixer, and combine them with the other ingredients. Add the salt, coconut flour, and melted butter, and mix until smooth.

Lay the chopped pecans on the bottom of the pie crust. Pour in the filling, and bake the pie for 20 minutes. Remove the pie from the oven, and garnish it with the pecan halves.

Put the pie back in the oven, and bake it for an additional 30 minutes. Allow the pie to cool, and refrigerate it until time to serve. It can be made a day ahead of time.

Serves 10

hunter-gatherer feast

At the very core of the Paleo lifestyle is the concept of hunting and foraging for food. Of course, in this day and age, very few people do either. The closest we get is picking wild raspberries or shooting a deer.

Our friend, Chuck, is an exception. He's a modern-day caveman and one of the most resourceful people we know. As his wife Tracy says, "If the world turns upside down tomorrow, you want Chuck in your cave." He's a fantastic hunter, and he gardens, fishes, and seems to be able to figure out just about anything else. When we first started jotting down ideas for *Gather*, we knew we wanted to spend an evening with Chuck and Tracy to enjoy some of the wild game Chuck had hunted in recent months.

When we started planning this menu, we quickly realized that Chuck not only had some fantastic cuts of meat for us, but he was also ea-

ger to impart some excellent cooking knowledge for preparing game meat. He provided much of the inspiration and insight for these dishes.

The elk he shared with us for this feast was shot on a ranch in New Mexico that is owned by Ted Turner. The venison originated in Nebraska, but Chuck gets a few locally every year. We even got our hands on a special cut of smoked elk loin, which was incredibly tasty!

For the foraged portion of this meal, we visited a local boutique grocery store called Wild Purveyors. We selected some locally cultivated mushrooms, which are often foraged in warmer months. They also had wild pears from a local orchard tree.

All in all, it was a fantastic evening: Chuck regaled us with his hunting stories as we enjoyed our delicious meal.

menu

. . . .

Sweet and Tangy Venison Meatballs

Wild Mushroom Soup

Apple-Scented Venison Roast

Grilled Elk Chops with Port Wine Reduction

Petite Potato Trio

Crème Brûlée

Shopping and Preparation

For this menu, we were able to dig through a chest-style freezer of game meat for most of our shopping! Hunting season is the perfect time to host a dinner for any friends who enjoy game. Low and slow cooking is best for venison or elk roasts. This lean meat can be quite tough, so the longer it cooks and marinates in aromatic juices, the better.

For this menu, we used some of the wild pears to decorate our table and played with soft green and beige for the table setting, using colors that made us think of the outdoors. We also used simple butcher's twine as napkin holders. The meal was elegant, but it still had a homey feel when we combined the earth tones and simple decorations with a formal dining room.

Three days ahead

If you're cooking game meat, it will most likely be frozen and packed away in a giant freezer. So, today, take any frozen meat out to thaw. You can also purchase any remaining items, and be sure you have all of your produce.

One day ahead

Start your roast in the slow cooker, marinate your ground meat, and make the sauce for your meatballs. Make the soup, and allow it to chill in the refrigerator overnight. You can also make your dessert ahead of time.

The day of the dinner

Most of your meal will be slow cooked, so today will involve finishing touches. Bake the meatballs, and let them simmer in their sauce. Let your soup simmer most of the day as well so that it's ready in time for serving. As your guests are arriving, put the potatoes in the oven to roast, and preheat the grill for the elk. Finishing the last bit of cooking while your guests are munching on appetizers will flow perfectly into dinner.

Gather // Dinner n°13

"hunter-gatherer"

first
smoked elk loin with wild pear
sweet and tangy venison meatballs
stuffed crimini mushrooms
with fried quail eggs

soup
wild mushroom soup

main
apple scented venison roast
grilled elk chops with port wine reduction

side
petite potato trio
steamed green beans with black truffle salt

dessert
creme brulee with raspberries

sweet and tangy venison meatballs

This delicious appetizer is what many would call a hunter's version of Swedish meatballs. It's easy to prepare ahead of time and keep warm in a crockpot. When we entertain, it's all about finding ways to streamline the dinner, and an appetizer like this one is just the ticket.

2 pounds ground venison

1 1/2 shallots, minced

2 cloves garlic, minced

1 tablespoon chocolate raspberry
balsamic vinegar*

2 tablespoons coconut aminos

Salt and pepper to taste

3 tablespoons bacon fat

Sauce

1 tablespoon duck fat

1/4 large onion, diced

8 ounces crushed pineapple

15 ounces tomato sauce (no salt added)

Salt and pepper to taste

2 tablespoons chocolate raspberry
balsamic vinegar

1 teaspoon maple sugar

*If you don't have chocolate raspberry balsamic vinegar, you may substitute standard balsamic vinegar.

Combine the ground venison, shallots, garlic, balsamic vinegar, coconut aminos, salt, and pepper in a large mixing bowl. Refrigerate the mixture overnight to allow the flavors to blend.

On the day of the dinner, add three tablespoons of bacon fat to the meat, and mix evenly. Preheat your oven to 350 degrees. Form the meat into roughly 1-inch balls, and place them on a parchment-lined baking sheet. Bake the meatballs for 25 minutes.

In a medium-sized saucepan, sauté the onion in the duck fat over medium heat. When the onion is translucent, add the pineapple, tomato sauce, salt, pepper, balsamic vinegar, and maple sugar to the saucepan. Simmer the mixture until the meatballs finish baking. Add the meatballs to the sauce, and stir to combine. You can keep the sauce and meatballs warm in a small crockpot or over low flame until time to serve.

Serves 10

wild mushroom soup

A great little grocery store called Wild Purveyors just opened in Pittsburgh. Tom and Cavan, the store owners, have been foraging for mushrooms and other edible plants for more than ten years. We were floored by all of the amazing mushrooms they had when we stopped in. For our wild mushroom soup, we like to use maitake, shiitake, and criminis for their varied textures and complementary flavors.

1 tablespoon duck fat

5 large carrots, chopped

1 head celery, chopped

1 green onion stalk, sliced

1 clove garlic, minced

Salt and pepper to taste

2 cups maitake mushrooms, cubed

1 cup crimini mushrooms, sliced

1 cup shiitake mushrooms, sliced

9 cups chicken stock

1 tablespoon fresh parsley

1 tablespoon fresh tarragon, minced

In a large cast iron skillet, add the duck fat, and sauté the carrots and celery over medium-high heat for 3 minutes. Add the green onion, and sauté for another minute. Add the garlic, and sauté for an additional minute. Sprinkle the vegetables with salt and pepper to taste.

Pour the vegetables into a large soup pot, and return the skillet to the flame, reduce to medium heat, and add the maitake mushrooms. Lightly sauté them, and then, add the maitake mushrooms to the soup pot.

Add the crimini and shiitake mushrooms to the skillet, season them with salt and pepper, and sauté them until the mushrooms soften slightly. Add the remaining mushrooms to the soup pot.

Cover the vegetables and mushrooms with chicken stock, and raise the flame to medium-high heat. Cover the soup, and bring it to a boil. Reduce the heat to low, add the parsley and tarragon, and cover. Simmer the soup for 2-4 hours. Season with additional salt and pepper, if needed, before serving.

Serves 10

apple-scented venison roast

Venison, particularly the roast, tends to be a very lean cut of meat. Slow cooking lean (and otherwise tough) cuts of meat is the best route to tenderness. The other benefit of using a slow cooker is the ability to get this dish underway long before your guests arrive.

1 pound hot Italian venison sausage, ground
    (or pork sausage)
2 tablespoons beef tallow
4 pound venison roast*
Salt and pepper to taste
1 cup beef broth
1 large vidalia onion, chopped
1 Granny Smith apple, chopped
1 tablespoon arrowroot flour

*If you cannot find venison, you can use a beef or bison roast instead.

In a large skillet, pan-sear the hot Italian sausage 1 minute per side. Place the browned sausage into a 6-quart crockpot and set it aside.

In the same skillet, add 1 tablespoon of beef tallow, and sear the venison roast 1-2 minutes per side, seasoning with salt and pepper, until evenly browned. Place the seared roast into the crockpot, making sure that some of the sausage is on top of the roast. Turn the crockpot to low heat, and pour in the beef broth. Cook the roast for 3 1/2 hours.

After the 3 1/2 hours, in a skillet, add the additional beef tallow, and sauté the onion and apple until the onion is translucent. Add the apple and onion to the crockpot. Allow the roast to cook 4 more hours. After a total of 7 1/2 hours, use a ladle to remove the excess stock if juices have accumulated from the roast. You should be able to fill a 24-ounce jar with excess juices and still have plenty in the crockpot for the roast to continue to cook.

After 9-10 hours, remove the roast from the crockpot, and allow it to cool completely. Slice the roast against the grain, place it back in the crockpot with the sausage, onion, and apple, and refrigerate it overnight.

The following day, bring the roast back up to room temperature, and warm it in the crockpot until serving time.

Pour the jar of excess juices into a heavy saucepan to warm, adding one tablespoon of arrowroot flour while whisking to thicken it for gravy.

Serves 10

grilled elk chops with port wine reduction

Grilling elk, much like any other cut of lean meat, is a simple process. Use the highest heat you can to quickly deliver a good sear. Then, back off the heat to finish cooking. The addition of the port wine reduction to this dish adds tremendous depth to the flavor of the elk.

To make the port wine reduction, add the butter to a skillet, and sauté the shallot until soft. Add 1/8 cup of the port wine to the skillet along with the rosemary. Cook until the liquid evaporates. Add the beef stock and the remaining 1 cup of port wine. Boil the mixture, stirring occasionally, until it reduces to approximately 1 1/2 cups of liquid. Strain the liquid into a small saucepan.

Heat a grill to high heat. Sear the elk steaks for 3-4 minutes per side, yielding medium-rare meat. Let the steaks rest for 5-10 minutes, and serve topped with the port wine reduction.

Serves 10

Port Wine Reduction

    2 tablespoons grass-fed butter

    1 shallot, finely diced

    1 1/8 cups port wine

    1 sprig rosemary

    1 quart beef stock

    Black pepper

10 elk steaks, about 6-8 ounces each*

*If you cannot find elk steaks, you can substitute another variety of red meat.

petite potato trio

There is something incredibly satisfying about a meal with meat and potatoes. It seems to evoke a deep-seated primal response from within. This trio of locally cultivated potatoes was the perfect accompaniment to our main courses of venison and elk.

1/2 pound fingerling white potatoes

1/2 pound fingerling sweet potatoes

1/2 pound small blue potatoes

1 tablespoon duck fat

Salt and pepper to taste

1/8 cup fresh thyme

1 tablespoon garlic powder

1 tablespoon onion powder

Preheat your oven to 400 degrees. Rinse and lightly scrub the white, sweet, and blue potatoes. Slice the potatoes in half, and place them in a baking dish.

In a small saucepan, melt the duck fat, and toss it with the potatoes. Sprinkle salt and pepper to taste over the potatoes. Add the fresh thyme, garlic powder, and onion powder, and toss.

Roast the potatoes for 35 minutes or until soft and the edges become golden.

Serves 10

crème brulée

We fell in love with Crème Brulée during our time in the Bahamas. In fact, we had just returned from that trip when we created this dinner. This light and sweet dessert is a nice finish to an otherwise hearty meal.

1 quart heavy cream
1 vanilla bean
1 cup maple sugar
6 egg yolks

Butane kitchen torch

Pour the heavy cream into a medium-sized saucepan. Slice the vanilla bean down the center, and scrape out the seeds using the knife. Place the vanilla seeds and the pod in the saucepan. Cook the vanilla cream over medium heat until it comes to a boil. Remove the pan from the heat, and allow the cream to cool for 15 minutes.

While the cream is cooling, in a medium-sized mixing bowl, whisk half a cup of the maple sugar with the egg yolks. When the vanilla cream has cooled, pour it into the mixing bowl while whisking it with the sugar and egg yolk mixture.

Preheat your oven to 350 degrees. Pour equal amounts of the mixture into 10 3-ounce ramekins. Make a "bain-marie" by placing the ramekins in a rimmed baking dish filled with water until it reaches halfway to the rims of the ramekins. Bake the crème brûlées for 45-50 minutes until they set up, yet still tremble in the center when lightly shaken. Cool them for a minimum of 1 hour in the refrigerator prior to serving. You may make these up to one day in advance.

Just before serving, evenly sprinkle the remaining maple sugar over the tops of the ramekins. Using a kitchen torch, caramelize the sugar on the top of each at a range of 3 inches from the surface, using a brisk circular motion. The sugar will bead up and melt together, forming a delicate crust. Allow the crème brûlées to cool slightly before serving.

Serves 10

birthday celebration

Birthdays are the milestones we all have in common. For some, they can sneak up or pass without fanfare. For others, they're a serious "to-do." Somewhere in the middle lies the type of birthday celebration most of us have: A day of kicking back and doing what we want. That, of course, means having our cake and eating it too.

For people following a Paleo lifestyle, the foods that are usually associated with celebrations can also be seriously detrimental to our health. Our goal with this menu was to lay out an entire birthday celebration that wouldn't feel like a compromise. The cake tastes like a cake, the burgers have buns, and the crackers with dip taste just like their conventional cousins.

This particular menu has a nice combination of items you can prepare ahead, as well as recipes to make right before the party. At the center of any birthday party is the cake. Fortunately, this cake recipe can be made in advance to avoid the pressure of rushing. The other make-ahead dish is the spinach and artichoke dip (along with the crackers), which will make setting up the early part of the party easy. All that will be left is cooking the sliders and frying (or heating up) the chicken nuggets.

When it comes time to celebrate a birthday, it will be an unforgettable day for all who attend.

menu

. . . .

Spinach and Artichoke Dip
with Herb Crackers

Pork Sliders and Veggie Sliders

Chicken Nuggets
with Honey Mustard

Checkerboard Cake

Shopping and Preparation

Whether you're young or old, a birthday party should be full of color and excitement. When we think of birthday parties, we remember running around with our friends, munching on chips and dip, chicken nuggets, and other finger foods. With flavors everyone can enjoy, this party menu is great for any child or adult birthday.

We used as much color as we could from balloons to plates to candles. Have fun with birthday decorations. You can't go too far when you're decorating for a loved one's birthday!

Two days ahead

Today, finish your food shopping. Gather any last-minute items you will need because tomorrow will be your day of cooking prep. Tonight, soak the cashews so that you can make the spinach and artichoke dip tomorrow.

One day ahead

Make the spinach and artichoke dip, the burger buns, the crackers, the cake, and the honey mustard. You can also grate all of the veggies for the veggie burgers. These items can be chilled overnight.

The day of the party

Decorate with the balloons, flowers, and party favors. Frost the cake several hours before the party, and keep it in the refrigerator to chill. Before your guests arrive, fry the chicken nuggets, and bake the burgers. As your guests arrive, finish plating the dishes so that your spread is ready for dining.

spinach and artichoke dip with herb crackers

This creamy spinach and artichoke dip uses soaked, raw cashews as a base instead of sour cream. It's the perfect party food for those who are allergic or avoiding dairy!

In a medium-sized mixing bowl, cover the cashews with filtered water, and soak them in the refrigerator overnight. The following day, drain the cashews, and place them in a food processor or high-speed blender. Pour in enough filtered water to just cover the cashews. Blend them until smooth. At this point, you will have "cashew cream."

In a medium-sized mixing bowl, add the cashew cream, nutritional yeast, onion powder, salt, pepper, and lemon juice.

In a large, heavy skillet, melt the coconut oil over medium heat. Add the artichoke hearts to the skillet, and sauté them for one minute. Add the minced garlic and spinach, and continue to sauté them for 5-7 minutes. Mash and chop the artichoke hearts with a silicone scraper or spoon as you sauté them. Let the mixture cool. Then, stir it together with the cashew cream. Refrigerate it until serving time.

Preheat your oven to 350 degrees. In a large mixing bowl, combine the almond flour, tapioca flour, salt, garlic powder, dried thyme, dried sage, and black pepper. Stir to combine. Pour in the melted coconut oil, and stir again. Pour in the eggs, and stir again until the batter is thoroughly combined. Dust with additional tapioca flour, and form the batter into a ball. Dust a large piece of parchment paper with tapioca flour, and place the dough onto the paper. Flatten the dough with your hands, and cover it with an additional sheet of parchment paper. Roll the dough into a large sheet of about 1/8-inch thick. Score the dough with a pizza cutter or knife, and bake the crackers for 15-18 minutes.

Remove the crackers from the oven, allow them to cool, and break them apart into individual crackers. These crackers are best made in two batches, removing excess dough from the first batch and repeating the process again to make the second batch.

Serves 10

2 cups raw cashews

Filtered water

1 tablespoon nutritional yeast*

1 tablespoon onion powder

Salt and pepper to taste

1 tablespoon fresh lemon juice

1 tablespoon coconut oil

28 ounces artichoke hearts (2 cans)

3 cloves garlic, minced

5 cups, fresh raw spinach, chopped

Crackers

    2 cups blanched almond flour

    1/4 cup tapioca flour

    1 teaspoon salt

    1 teaspoon garlic powder

    1 teaspoon dried thyme

    1 teaspoon dried sage

    1 teaspoon black pepper

    1/4 cup coconut oil, melted

    2 eggs, whisked

*We use Lewis Labs Brewers Yeast, because it is grown on sugar beets and not beer

pork sliders and veggie sliders

Bill's aunt and cousin avoid animal protein, so we tried our best to make a real veggie burger. This burger was made with vegetables and some egg, not like traditional veggie burgers that use soy and beans. For the meat eaters in the house, we served up some tasty pork sausage sliders.

Buns
   3 cups blanched almond flour
   1 cup hot water
   2 tablespoons apple cider vinegar
   1/4 cup arrowroot flour
   3 eggs, separated
   2 teaspoons gluten-free baking powder
   1 teaspoon onion powder
   1 teaspoon garlic powder
   1 teaspoon salt
   1 teaspoon pepper
   1 teaspoon dried rosemary
   Sesame seeds

Pork sliders
   2 pounds ground pork
   1/2 tablespoon salt
   1/2 tablespoon pepper
   1 tablespoon garlic powder
   1 tablespoon onion powder
   1/2 tablespoon oregano
   1 tablespoon fennel seeds
   2 teaspoons paprika

Veggie sliders
   3 large carrots
   1 medium sweet potato (white)
   1/4 medium onion
   2 small zucchini squash
   1 egg, whisked
   1/2 cup arrowroot flour
   1 tablespoon coconut aminos
   1 teaspoon salt
   1 teaspoon pepper

For the buns, preheat your oven to 375 degrees. In a large mixing bowl, combine two cups of the blanched almond flour, the hot water, and the apple cider vinegar. Fold the ingredients together using a wooden spoon. Add the baking powder, onion powder, garlic powder, salt, pepper, and dried rosemary. Fold all of the ingredients together.

In a separate small bowl, whisk the egg yolks, and add them to the dough. Add the remaining cup of almond flour, as well as the arrowroot flour, and stir to combine the ingredients.

In a separate mixing bowl, whip the egg whites with a hand mixer until stiff. Carefully fold the egg whites into the dough. Drop 1/4 cup of the batter onto a parchment-lined baking sheet, smoothing out the dough into the shape of a bun. Repeat with the remaining dough. Sprinkle the dough with sesame seeds, and bake it for 20-25 minutes.

For the pork sliders, preheat your oven to 350 degrees. In a large mixing bowl, combine the ground pork, salt, pepper, garlic powder, onion powder, oregano, fennel seeds, and paprika. Mix the meat with your hands until it is evenly seasoned. Place 3-ounce sliders on a parchment-lined baking sheet, and bake them for 30-35 minutes.

For the veggies sliders, preheat your oven to 375 degrees. Using the shredder blade from a food processor or a box grater, grate the carrots, sweet potato, and onion. Place them in a large mixing bowl. Then, grate the zucchini, and using a clean dish towel or paper towel, wring out any excess water from the shredded zucchini.

Add the zucchini to the mixing bowl, as well as the whisked egg, arrowroot flour, coconut aminos, salt, and pepper. Combine all ingredients using your hands, and form the veggie "meat" into small patties (about the size of your palm). Place them on a parchment-lined baking sheet, and bake them for 35 minutes or until crispy on the outside and set on the inside.

Serves 10

chicken nuggets with honey mustard

Arrowroot flour makes a great crispy "breading" for homemade chicken nuggets. At first bite, these nuggets take me right back to summers at the pool munching down on fried chicken nuggets during adult swim.

Honey Mustard

    1 cup homemade mayonnaise

        1/3 cup coconut oil, melted

        1/3 cup sesame oil

        1/3 cup extra-virgin olive oil

        1 egg

        1 tablespoon brown mustard

        1 tablespoon lemon juice

        Pinch of salt

    2 tablespoons brown mustard

    1/2 teaspoon lemon juice

    1 tablespoon pure maple syrup

1 1/2 pounds boneless, skinless chicken thighs

2 eggs, whisked

1 cup arrowroot flour

1 tablespoon salt

5-10 cups pure lard, tallow, or coconut oil

To make the mayonnaise, melt the coconut oil in a glass liquid measuring cup with a spout. Allow the coconut oil to cool enough to pour the other cold oils into the cup. Stir in the sesame oil and olive oil. In a food processor or high-speed blender, blend the egg, brown mustard, lemon juice, and pinch of salt. Drizzle in the oil mixture at a very slow trickle (taking 3-4 minutes for the entire cup of oil). Continue to process until the mayonnaise has reached a desirable consistency.

In a medium-sized mixing bowl, stir together the mayonnaise, the additional brown mustard, lemon juice, and maple syrup. Stir until combined, and refrigerate until ready to use.

Cut the chicken thighs into 1-inch pieces. In a medium-sized mixing bowl, whisk the two eggs, and add the arrowroot flour and salt a little at a time until you achieve a thick, almost glue-like texture. Place the chicken chunks into the bowl, and toss them to evenly coat with the slurry.

In a fryer, cast iron skillet, or deep-rimmed Dutch oven, heat the lard (or other fat of your choice) on medium-high heat. The optimal oil temperature will be in the 300-330-degree range. Fry the chicken pieces, in small batches, for 7-10 minutes or until the pieces have a golden brown crust and are cooked through to the center.

Serves 10

checkerboard cake

No birthday celebration would be complete without a fantastically indulgent birthday cake. This checkerboard cake is a family tradition for milestone birthdays and is certain to make any birthday boy or girl feel extra special.

Cake Batter

- 1 cup grass-fed butter, softened
- 1 cup maple sugar
- 3 eggs
- 1 cup coconut milk (full fat)
- 1/2 teaspoon salt
- 4 teaspoons gluten-free baking powder
- 2 1/2 cups blanched almond flour
- 1/2 cup arrowroot flour
- 1/2 vanilla bean pod, seeds only
- 1 teaspoon pure vanilla extract
- 1/2 of the batter will use
    - 2 tablespoons cocoa powder

"Butter" Cream Frosting

- 1 cup palm shortening
- 3 cups organic powdered sugar
- 1 cup heavy cream
- 1 teaspoon pure vanilla extract
- Pinch of salt

Checkerboard Cake Mold (available at kitchen stores)

Preheat your oven to 350 degrees. In a standing mixer, cream the butter and maple sugar. Add the eggs one at a time, followed by the coconut milk, salt, and baking powder. Add the almond flour, one cup at a time, blending after each cup. Add the remaining half cup of almond flour and half cup of arrowroot flour, and blend until smooth, scraping down the sides of the mixing bowl as needed.

Grease three 9-inch round cake pans with butter, and line the bottom of the pans with parchment paper for easy removal. Pour half of the batter into a separate mixing bowl. Add the vanilla seeds to this half of the batter, and stir it with a wooden spoon. Add the vanilla extract and cocoa powder to the batter remaining in the standing mixer, and blend until smooth. Pour the batter into two different piping bags, and pipe even circles of batter, following a checkerboard guide. Fill two cake pans with two circles of chocolate batter and a vanilla circle of batter (see the images on the opposite page). Fill one cake pan with two circles of vanilla batter and one circle of chocolate batter in the center.

Bake for 25-30 minutes or until a toothpick inserted into the batter comes out clean. Remove the cakes from the oven, and set them aside to cool. Refrigerate overnight if you're making this cake a day ahead of time.

In a standing mixer, cream the palm shortening and one cup of organic powdered sugar. Add the remaining two cups of sugar one at a time, blending after each cup. Add the heavy cream, vanilla extract, and salt. Blend until smooth and fluffy.

To frost the cake, smooth a layer of frosting in between each layer of cake, alternating the different chocolate and vanilla layers, and lightly smooth a layer of frosting over the entire cake. If the frosting starts to melt while you are trying to smooth it out, place the cake and the bowl of frosting in the refrigerator for 5 minutes. Then, finish frosting the cake.

You can also make this recipe without powdered sugar by using 2-3 cups of palm shortening and 1 cup of maple sugar.

Serves 10

winter holiday

As the days get shorter when the holidays approach, we start to crave comfort foods. To us, nothing says comfort food more than a house filled with the scent of our favorite dishes. Slow-roasted meats, grain-free treats baking in the oven, and a multitude of side dishes are among the familiar smells of the season. We crave starchier, more filling foods, and enjoy the crisp air as the first snowflakes begin to fall. What could be more charming (some would say, romantic) than getting all cozy, popping some bacon chocolate chip cookies in the oven, and curling up on the couch to watch *Miracle on 34th Street?*

Above all else, though, the holidays are a cherished time with family. Almost all of our traditions seem to revolve around food. Some of our favorite holiday recipes have been passed down from generation to generation. Anyone who has our first book, *Make It Paleo*, knows all about our family recipes. Pumpkin Chiffon Pie, anyone?

When you're planning a gathering during the holidays, however, there is already the undeniable stress of the season with people rushing around buying presents and worrying about how to make everyone happy. It can make holiday entertaining difficult. To keep it easy, we always select dishes that require a bit less effort but, at the same time, don't sacrifice taste or presentation.

Select a time that works well for most people, and keep the schedule for the dinner relaxed. If people want to bring dishes, let them, but don't require it. There are plenty of ideas throughout this book and on our website that will work in a pinch. Most of all, remember that the holidays are about family, not about executing a flawless dinner. The occasion will be the most enjoyable for your guests if you keep this in mind. In other words, just let go and enjoy the time with everyone.

menu

· ·

Winter Pomegranate Salad
with Fig Balsamic Vinaigrette

Candied Yams

Standing Rib Roast with Horseradish Sauce

Roasted Green and Purple Cabbage

Yorkshire Puddings

Sour Cream Coffee Cake

Shopping and Preparation

Christmas dinner can be just as time-consuming and stressful as Thanksgiving dinner. Christmas and Thanksgiving are the two main holidays of the year that have a strong focus on a big meal with family. Every year, Bill's aunt spends a week preparing for her Christmas dinner, and it's phenomenal every time! You can see all the hard work she puts into the dinner; everything is beautiful and well thought out.

Winter holidays are another time when it can be fun to involve other family members in the cooking. We like to minimize stress by making recipes that we can "set and forget," such as roasting dishes. You may only have to check on these items a few times through cooking, so you can focus on setting the table and celebrating with loved ones while the main dishes roast.

Five days ahead

This is a big holiday. Your dinner should be carefully thought out and thoroughly planned. Make sure all of your good table linens are clean, and get your good china, silverware, and glassware ready. Tree trimmings, pine cones, jingle bells, and even tree ornaments can all be placed on your table as decorations. Most homes are already beautifully decorated, so you may not need much to set the mood for this festive meal.

Three days ahead

Today, you can finish your shopping. All produce can be purchased, as well as your roast. Be sure that you have all items on hand for the coffee cake, and purchase any last-minute holiday favors that you may offer to your guests.

One day before the dinner

Make the coffee cake, as well as the candied yams and horseradish sauce, and keep them chilled in the refrigerator overnight. Also, set your dining room table.

The day of the dinner

Two hours before dinner, put the roast and the cabbage dish in the oven. As your guests arrive, warm the yams, and plate the salad. As soon as the rib roast comes out of the oven, pop the Yorkshire puddings in for a quick bake while the roast rests.

winter pomegranate salad with fig balsamic vinaigrette

The sweet crunch of pomegranate seeds is a delightful surprise in this salad. With citrus coming into season around the holidays, this salad is a great way to use the abundant fruit in a festive way.

10 cups mixed salad greens

3 Satsuma oranges (or 4 clementines)

1/4 cup raw walnuts, chopped

1/2 cup pomegranate seeds

Dressing

    1/3 cup fig balsamic vinegar*

    1/4 cup extra-virgin olive oil

    Salt and pepper to taste

In a large serving platter or bowl, toss the salad greens along with the peeled and sectioned Satsuma oranges, chopped walnuts, and pomegranate seeds.

In a separate small mixing bowl, whisk together the balsamic vinegar, olive oil, salt, and pepper. Toss the salad with the dressing just before serving.

Serves 8

* If you do not have fig balsamic vinegar, you may substitute with any fruity balsamic vinegar.

8 jewel or garnet yams (sweet potatoes)

1 pineapple, core removed

1/2 cup grass-fed butter

1/4 cup maple syrup

candied yams

This is Grandy Kyp's recipe for candied yams. We enjoyed them last year for Thanksgiving, and I was thrilled to find out that they were completely "Paleo-friendly"! For our winter holiday dinner, we decided to recreate this recipe from memory. The yams turned out wonderful and just as I remembered them.

Preheat your oven to 425 degrees. Cut the ends off of the sweet potatoes, and poke each in several spots with a fork. Bake the sweet potatoes for 1 hour. Then, allow them to cool. When they are cool, peel the skin off of them.

Chop pineapple and place in a food processor. Pulse until finely diced. In a medium-sized saucepan, add the crushed pineapple, butter, and maple syrup. Bring the mixture to a boil, and reduce by half. Pour the topping over the yams, and serve.

Serves 8

standing rib roast with horseradish sauce

Every year, we join Bill's grandparents for an early Christmas dinner at their country club in Ohio. While there are many fantastic dishes to choose from, the prime rib with horseradish sauce is a favorite of ours. Making this at home for your holiday dinner is an elegant and delicious addition to the meal!

4 rib standing rib roast, frenched

1/4 cup grass-fed butter

Salt and pepper to taste

2 tablespoons fresh thyme

Horseradish Sauce

    8 ounces crème fraîche

    1/3 cup + 1 tablespoon pure horseradish

    Pinch of salt

    1 teaspoon ground black pepper

    1 teaspoon onion powder

    1/4 teaspoon dried dill weed

This dish starts with a trip to your local butcher. When you speak with your butcher, be sure to ask for the loin end of the roast, as the leanness of the meat is preferable for this recipe. If you wish, for a fancier presentation, you can have the bones "Frenched" as seen in the photos. This recipe works best for roasts of 3 ribs or more with each rib serving approximately 2 people.

Bring the prime rib to room temperature at least 30 minutes prior to cooking. Preheat your oven to 450 degrees. Place the roast fat-side up in a roasting pan.

In a small saucepan, melt the butter, and pour it over the prime rib, ensuring even coverage. Season the meat with salt and pepper, and top it with the thyme. Roast the prime rib for 15 minutes. Then, lower the temperature to 350 degrees, and cook it for an additional 45 minutes. Using a meat thermometer, monitor the internal temperature of the meat. When the prime rib reaches an internal temperature of 120, remove it from the oven. Allow the meat to rest for 30 minutes before serving.

In a medium-sized mixing bowl, pour the crème fraîche, add the horseradish, and stir until combined. Stir in the salt, black pepper, onion powder, and dried dill weed. Then, cover the mixture, and refrigerate it at least 30 minutes prior to serving or overnight.

Serves 8

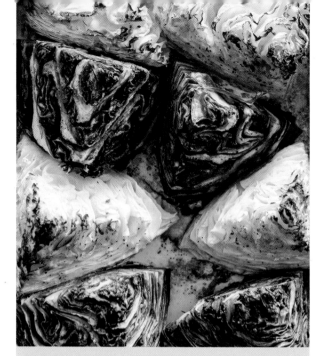

roasted green and purple cabbage

This dish is fun, festive, and incredibly colorful. It's quite simple to make and an easy way to get some beautiful food on the table with little stress.

Preheat the oven to 400 degrees. Peel the outer layer away from the green and purple cabbages. Cut the cabbages into wedges, and place them in a baking dish.

In a small saucepan, melt the butter, and pour it over the cabbage. Sprinkle the cabbage with salt, pepper, rosemary, thyme, and sage. Bake the cabbage for about 45-60 minutes, and serve.

Serves 8

1 medium green cabbage
1 medium purple cabbage
1/3 cup grass-fed butter
Salt and pepper to taste
1 tablespoon dried rosemary
1 tablespoon dried thyme
1 tablespoon dried sage

yorkshire puddings

These light and fluffy pastry-like rolls have been made in England for centuries. They were originally made alongside roasts, incorporating fat drippings into a flour-based batter. The ingredients in this version are a far cry from the traditional recipe, though the result is the same—delicious little biscuits that are perfect with a holiday feast.

In a medium-sized mixing bowl, whisk together the almond flour, arrowroot flour, salt, pepper, eggs, and heavy cream. The batter can be refrigerated up to 4 hours prior to cooking. If the batter separates, whisk it again before baking.

Preheat your oven to 450 degrees. Grease each muffin cup with the lard, and fill each cup 3/4 of the way to the top with the batter. Bake for 20 minutes or until golden brown on top.

Serves 8

1 cup almond flour

2 tablespoons arrowroot flour

1/2 teaspoon salt

1/2 teaspoon pepper

3 eggs

1 cup heavy cream

6 tablespoons lard

sour cream coffee cake

This coffee cake recipe is a Staley family Christmas tradition. Every year, my father makes his sour cream coffee cake on Christmas Eve before the family goes to the candlelight church service. Then, on Christmas morning, we stick it in the oven to warm while everyone opens their presents. This grain-free version of his famously good coffee cake is worthy of a Christmas day celebration. Make enough to enjoy leftovers because it's just as good the next day.

1 cup grass-fed butter, softened

1 1/2 cups maple sugar

4 eggs

2 teaspoons pure vanilla extract

1 1/2 teaspoons baking soda

1/4 teaspoon salt

2 1/2 cups almond flour

1/4 cup arrowroot flour

1 cup sour cream

Unsalted grass-fed butter to grease
    the springform pan

Topping
    1/2 cup chopped walnuts
    2 teaspoons cinnamon
    1/2 cup coconut sugar

Glaze
    2 1/2 tablespoons water
    1 tablespoon grass-fed butter
    1 1/2 cups organic powdered cane sugar
    Pinch of salt
    2 teaspoons finely ground espresso

Preheat your oven to 350 degrees. In a medium-sized mixing bowl, stir together the butter and maple sugar. Add the eggs one at a time, and continue to mix. Add the vanilla extract.

In a separate mixing bowl, blend the baking soda, salt, almond flour, and arrowroot flour together. Combine the dry ingredients with the wet ingredients alternately with the sour cream, adding a little bit at a time. The batter will be thick.

In a separate small mixing bowl, stir together the chopped walnuts, cinnamon, and coconut sugar for the topping.

Using unsalted butter, generously grease a fluted bundt springform cake pan. Pour a small amount of the topping mixture into the bottom of the pan. Pour about 1/3 of the batter into the pan, and smooth it into an even layer. Layer 1/3 of the topping over the batter. Continue layering in thirds, finally ending with topping on top, which will ultimately be the bottom of the cake.

Bake the coffee cake for 55 minutes. When the cake is done, allow it to cool. After it has cooled, carefully separate it from the springform pan, and place it on a plate or cake stand with the fluted side up.

Make the glaze by heating the water and butter in a saucepan until it starts to bubble. Sift the powdered sugar into a medium-sized mixing bowl, stirring in the salt and ground espresso. Pour the water and hot butter over the dry ingredients, and whisk until smooth. Drizzle the glaze over the top of the cake, and serve.

Serves 10

new year's eve cocktail party

New Year's celebrations are the ultimate "reset." Once a year, we all get to forget about the past and focus on the good that lies ahead. No matter how you choose to celebrate at this time of year, the overflow of optimism is enough to get almost anyone in the holiday spirit.

Each year, we make an effort to get together with friends and family for this special evening. We also try to get into the city to see the fireworks and enjoy First Night festivities. This year, we were able to do it all. Our friends, Jill and Brian, offered up their penthouse apartment in downtown Pittsburgh for a gathering of friends to ring in 2013.

We developed a nice menu of hors d'oeuvres for the evening that were easy to share, pass around, and nibble. After all, cocktail parties are about mingling, having a drink, chatting with your friends, and, of course, scrumptious food. We kept the food light and fun, and we kicked everything off with the two hot dishes, the butternut squash soup shooters, and the "pigs in a blanket." These dishes are best served hot, so you should serve them as soon as your guests arrive. The remaining dishes can be passed around or set out because they don't have to stay warm. This plan helps you enjoy the evening too!

To recreate this party for your celebration, prepare the food ahead of time. Purchase a good quality champagne (or sparkling wine) and party crackers or sparklers, if you wish. We went for an elegant look with a silver and black theme. Details, such as the sage leaf tied to the soup shooters, will make the evening especially memorable. And, of course, with any cocktail party, don't forget the wine charms so that people don't confuse their drinks!

menu

Butternut Squash Soup Shooters

Pigs in a Blanket

Crostini with Goat Cheese and Fig Compote

Antipasti Skewers

Mini Chocolate Martinis

Shopping and Preparation

Your guests will gasp when they see grain-free pigs in a blanket, and they will be sure to forget that the toasted crostini isn't made from white flour.

Three days ahead

Today is the day to finish your shopping. You can purchase all produce today, as well as party favors and champagne. New Year's Eve is all about sparkles, so don't be afraid to use decorations that are a little over the top.

One day ahead

Make the butternut squash soup, the French bread for the crostini, the fig compote, and the mini chocolate martinis. You can also make the antipasti skewers and keep them chilled in the refrigerator until tomorrow. Roast the red peppers for the antipasti skewers, and marinate overnight.

The day of the party

Today is going to be all about finishing touches and final food prep. Make sure your home is decorated for the party and that your bar is set up before you finish the cooking. The soup can simmer for a few hours so that it's ready when your guests arrive. Slice and toast the crostini, and bake the pigs in a blanket. After your guests have had their fill of the food, awe them with their mini martini desserts.

butternut squash soup shooters

These cute little soup shooters are a great start to any cocktail party. Garnished with a thin strip of crispy bacon, everyone will be eager to start the party with a shot of this delicious and creamy soup.

To make the chicken stock, place a chicken carcass and/or chicken backs in a slow cooker, along with sea salt and apple cider vinegar. Cover everything with filtered water, and cook on low for 16-24 hours. Once the broth is finished cooking, strain the broth to remove all bones This can also be made in a pressure cooker in 1 hour on high pressure.

In a large soup pot, add the squash, carrots, onion, cinnamon, salt, black pepper, nutmeg, ginger, and four cups of chicken stock. Bring the soup to a boil over medium heat. Then, turn the heat down to low, cover the pot, and simmer the soup for 1 hour or until all vegetables are soft.

Purée the soup in a high-speed blender or food processor. Return the soup to the pot, and simmer it until serving time. If you're making the soup a day ahead, refrigerate it overnight, and start to reheat it an hour before serving. Serve the soup in 2-ounce shot glasses, and garnish it with crispy bacon slices.

Serves 10

4 cups chicken stock
   3 pounds chicken bones
   1 tablespoon sea salt
   1 tablespoon apple cider vinegar
5 cups butternut squash, peeled and cubed
2 large carrots, peeled and chopped
1/2 large onion
1 teaspoon cinnamon
1 teaspoon salt
1 teaspoon black pepper
1/4 teaspoon nutmeg
1/4 teaspoon ginger
3 strips bacon, cooked until crispy

pigs in a blanket

No cocktail party would be complete (at least in Pittsburgh) without cocktail weiners. These fun little "pigs in a blanket" are just as tasty as they are cute.

Pigs in a Blanket

- 1 1/2 cups blanched almond flour
- 1/2 cup arrowroot flour
- 1 teaspoon gluten-free baking powder
- 1/2 teaspoon salt
- 1/2 teaspoon garlic powder
- 1/2 teaspoon onion powder
- 1 teaspoon black pepper
- 1/3 cup warm water
- 1 tablespoon apple cider vinegar
- 36 cocktail wieners (Wellshire brand)

Dip

- 1 cup spicy brown mustard
- 2 tablespoons horseradish

Preheat the oven to 350 degrees. In a medium-sized mixing bowl, combine 1 cup of the blanched almond flour, 1/4 cup of the arrowroot flour, the baking powder, salt, garlic powder, onion powder, and black pepper. Stir to combine. Add 1/3 cup warm water to the mixture, and lightly stir using a folding motion to combine the batter. Add the apple cider vinegar, and continue to stir. Add the remaining half cup of blanched almond flour, and combine. Dust with the remaining 1/4 cup of arrowroot flour to firm up the dough.

Using teaspoon-sized portions, lightly roll the dough into thin ovals, placing a cocktail wiener in the center and wrapping the dough around it in a ring shape. Place each cocktail wiener on a parchment-lined baking sheet, and bake for 35 minutes. Remove the pigs in a blanket from the oven, and turn the temperature up to 425 degrees. Place them back in the oven to brown for approximately 3 minutes.

In a small bowl, combine the spicy brown mustard with the horseradish as an accompanying dip. Refrigerate the horseradish mustard until serving time.

Serves 10

French Bread

3 cups blanched almond flour

1 cup arrowroot flour

1 teaspoon salt

2 teaspoons gluten-free baking powder

2/3 cup warm water

2 tablespoons apple cider vinegar

1 tablespoon maple syrup

1 egg white (for egg wash)

Fig Compote

1/2 cup dried black mission figs, chopped

1 cup chocolate raspberry balsamic
    vinegar*

1/2 teaspoon dried marjoram

Pinch of salt

2 tablespoons water

8 ounces soft goat cheese

Chopped chives for garnish

*If you cannot find chocolate raspberry balsamic, you can use regular balsamic vinegar.

crostini with goat cheese and fig compote

Unsuspecting guests may forget that they aren't eating "real" bread when they try this charming, grain-free toasted appetizer. This recipe is a bit involved to make but is well worth the effort.

Preheat your oven to 375 degrees. To make the French bread, in a large mixing bowl, pour 1 1/2 cups of almond flour. Add a half cup of arrowroot flour, the salt, and the baking powder. Stir the dry ingredients to combine.

Add 2/3 cup warm water to the dry ingredients, and lightly stir to combine. Use a folding motion to blend the batter. Add the apple cider vinegar and maple syrup, and continue to stir. Add the remaining 1 1/2 cups of almond flour to the dough, stir to combine, and dust with additional arrowroot flour (up to the remaining half cup), until the dough is firm enough to form into a loaf.

Split the dough into 2 equal portions. Dust a parchment-lined baking sheet with arrowroot flour. Form each half portion of the dough into a thin oval loaf on the baking sheet. Cut diagonal slits down the length of the bread loaf, and bake the loaves for 20 minutes.

Remove the loaves from the oven, and baste them with the egg wash. Then, bake them for 10 more minutes. Remove the loaves from the oven, and turn the oven temperature up to 400 degrees. Baste the loaves with the egg wash once more, and bake the loaves for a final 5 minutes at 400 degrees.

Allow the loaves to cool, and tightly wrap them with plastic wrap. Refrigerate the loaves until serving time.

To make the fig compote, in a medium-sized, heavy saucepan, add the chopped figs, balsamic vinegar, dried marjoram, and salt. Stir to combine all ingredients. Bring the mixture to a boil over medium heat. Then, turn the heat to low, and allow the mixture to cook at a low bubble for 25-30 minutes, stirring often until thickened. Add the 2 tablespoons of water, and stir. Remove the pan from the heat, and allow the compote to cool.

To plate the dish, slice 1/2-inch thick pieces from the loaves, and toast the pieces on a baking sheet at 425 degrees for 10-15 minutes or until lightly browned. Allow the pieces to cool. Then, spread goat cheese over the toast, and top with fig compote and chives.

Serves 10

antipasti skewers

These skewers are the perfect finger food for a party. With a nice balance of flavors, they complement other foods very well. Since ingredient quality is important to us, we roast and marinate our own red peppers for this dish.

4 red bell peppers

1 clove garlic, crushed

1 1/2 teaspoons red pepper flakes

1 teaspoon oregano

1 cup extra-virgin olive oil

8 ounces soppressata

14 ounces green olives

28 ounces artichoke hearts

Skewers

The day before making the skewers, place the red bell peppers on a rimmed baking sheet, and bake them at 450 degrees until the peppers start to develop dark spots on the skin (about 25-30 minutes). Rotate the peppers to blacken them evenly. Remove them from the oven, and allow the peppers to cool. Once the peppers have cooled, peel the skin away, and remove the seeds. Place the cleaned strips of pepper in a small mason jar. Add the crushed garlic, red pepper flakes, oregano, and olive oil. Keep the roasted red peppers refrigerated overnight.

Make each skewer with a piece of soppressata, an olive or two, a piece of artichoke heart, and a small slice of the red bell pepper.

Makes about 50-60 4-inch skewers

Serves 10

6 ounces dark chocolate (70%)

2 eggs

1 teaspoon pure vanilla extract

1 cup heavy cream

Garnish

　1/2 cup heavy cream*

　Cocoa powder

　Pineapple, cubed

　12 fresh cherries

12 mini-martini glasses or 2-ounce ramekins

Skewers

*For a non-dairy version, use full fat coconut milk in place of the heavy cream.

mini chocolate martinis

New Year's Eve celebrations are notorious for fancy cocktails. With these chocolate martinis, your guests will enjoy a non-alcoholic, yet decadent dessert "cocktail" that adds to the charm of the evening.

In a high-speed blender, blend the dark chocolate, eggs, and vanilla extract.

In a small saucepan, heat the heavy cream until scalding. You will see steam rising, but no bubbles. Add the scalded cream to the blender, and blend until smooth.

Pour the chocolate cream into each glass, dividing equally between the 12. Cover the glasses with plastic wrap, and refrigerate for at least 2 hours before serving.

To garnish, whip the heavy cream until stiff. Place the cream into a piping bag, and pipe a small dollop on each glass. Dust the cream with cocoa powder, and serve each glass with a skewer of a pineapple cube and cherry.

Serves 12

gratitude

From Bill:

A book of this scope and magnitude was an undertaking beyond the furthest stretches of our imaginations (and at times, sanity). We knew we wanted to write an entertaining cookbook about two years ago, and when we started to work on it in earnest about a year ago, we laid out a truly ambitious plan—seven months of shooting inspiring menus on location all over the country (and even in some other countries). To some extent, we achieved that, and somehow managed to grow our relationship with one another in the process. Just before we started to work on *Gather*, we got engaged. I'm truly lucky to have such an amazing partner in life, and I know Hay feels the same. We are blessed to get to do this together. *Gather* brought us so much closer, so we hope the love and care with which we created each menu is apparent. We had a lot of fun working on this book together. I want to thank my amazing, talented, loving, and ever-supportive partner in life, Hayley. My world is infinitely better with you in it. I love you, and I can't wait to become your husband this year.

From Hayley:

My mom always told me I was special and that I would do big things in life. I guess I always believed her but never really believed in myself enough to make anything happen. After I met Bill, I realized that he was my missing link. None of this would have been possible without him in my life. He makes me a better person, and I strive to work harder because of him. I still can't believe that we have accomplished this project together, and even though it

was tough at times, never once did we give up on each other. This book is alive and real because we created it together through support, love, and friendship. I'm eternally grateful that I have such an amazing partner in all aspects of life. If we can accomplish this, we can accomplish anything.

From both of us:

We received a tremendous amount of help, encouragement, and support throughout the production of *Gather*, so there are a lot of people to thank.

To our location hosts, who opened up their homes, kitchens, and schedules for us to shoot photos for this book: Bill and Nellie, Nellie and Chris, Terry and Cyndi, Alexa (twice), Emily and Scott, Mike and Natalie, Stacy and Matt, Brian and Jennifer, Erin and Beaver, Chuck and Tracy (twice), Michelle and Henry, Tony and Justine, Jill and Brian, and Sandy and Bryan. You allowed us to come into your homes, turn your kitchens upside down, and wreak a bit of havoc for a day, sometimes two! Sure, you got to eat the food, but we are in your debt far more than what one meal can pay back. Thank you all from the bottoms of our hearts for opening your doors and setting aside time to be a part of this crazy project. This book is beautiful because of your amazing homes.

To our families, who have stood in support of us over the last few years as we trek down a path few have taken before. Thank you for your steadfast belief in everything we do. We love you!

To Tony, we're lucky to have someone like you to share this journey with us. Thanks for putting your faith in our startup and for encouraging us to take our business up a notch in 2012. The depth of our gratitude cannot be measured for your friendship and involvement in our lives, both professionally and personally.

To Diane, our friend, fellow author, and business muse extraordinaire, it was an amazing honor working on *Practical Paleo* with you in 2012. At the time of us going to print (February, 2013), your book has been on the *New York Times Bestseller* list over 14 times! We couldn't be happier for you and your incredible successes!

To our dear friends who also happen to have amazing blogs and voices in the Paleo community, we are so grateful to see you "at the office" (online) every day. You make this job a whole lot of fun for us: Liz Wolfe, our friend since day one of joining the Paleo scene. George Bryant, who has impressed us with his big heart and meteoric rise in popularity. Michelle and Henry, and Stacy and Matt, who make running families, working full-time jobs, and writing amazing blogs look easy. And all our trusted friends in Pittsburgh and everywhere else who always give us encouragement and make us smile. You know who you are, and we are so grateful to have you in our lives.

A very special thank you to our partners: KitchenAid, Le Creuset, Wusthof, and Blendtec. Your top quality products keep our kitchen churning out great food with ease and enjoyment. It's a pleasure to stand behind your fantastic products. Thank you!

To Mark Sisson, who continues to touch countless lives in his mission to get the world healthy, we will never forget that we got our start from being featured on your website in 2010. Thank you for helping us and for writing the stellar foreword to *Make It Paleo*, our first cookbook.

To Justin and Paul at ShoFilms, who shot our incredible trailer for *Gather*. Justin accompanied us on a pair of shoots and captured the hidden magic of orchestrating our gatherings for this book. We are in awe of your talents, and are thankful we get the chance to work with you on several projects!

To Adam Milliron, who helped us shoot the gorgeous cover photo for *Gather*. We have never seen photographic genius at work quite like the day Adam helped us with our cover. Thank you for sharing your time and talent with us!

To Erich and Michele at Victory Belt, you are the real heroes in our lives because it was our first book that allowed us to take this from a hobby to a career. Thank you for taking a chance on two young Paleo food bloggers from Pittsburgh. Your faith in our vision makes this all worth doing because you allow our books to be published as we envision them. Thank you!

And finally, a big thank you to our fans and followers! We couldn't have done this without your support. Thank you so much!

dishes listed by course

Appetizers

Antipasti Skewers - 296
Avocado Cream Eggs - 72
Bacon-Wrapped Shrimp - 124
Butternut Squash Soup Shooters - 290
Carrots with Olive Tapenade Trio - 60
Crab-Stuffed Artichoke Bottoms - 170
Crostini with Goat Cheese and Fig Compote - 294
Cucumber and Salmon Bites - 60
Pigs in a Blanket - 292
Spiced Nuts with Rosemary and Thyme - 172
Spinach and Artichoke Dip with Herb Crackers - 258
Venison Meatballs, Sweet and Tangy - 240

Breakfast and Brunch

Cinnamon Maple Hot Cakes - 50
Eggs Benedict - 44
Pork Belly, Braised - 46

Desserts and Treats

Almond Cookies - 36
Apple Pie with a Lattice Crust - 132
Biscotti, Chocolate Chip - 114
Blackberry Cobbler with Vanilla Bean Ice Cream - 178
"Bleeding" Cupcakes - 210
Caramel Crab Apples - 214
Checkerboard Cake - 264
Coconut Flan (Flan de Coco) - 162
Coffee Cake, Sour Cream - 282
Crème Brûlée - 250
Flan de Coco (Coconut Flan) - 162
Gelato, Dark Chocolate - 116
Lemon Blueberry Muffins - 98

Meyer Lemon Tart - 82
Mini Chocolate Martinis - 298
Mummy Cookies - 212
Pecan Pie - 232
Pumpkin Torte with Cream Cheese Frosting and Caramel - 196
Scones, Cranberry and Orange - 62
Vanilla Bean Ice Cream - 178
Yorkshire Puddings - 280
Zucchini Bread - 64

Drinks

Affogato (French Press Coffee) - 116
Rooibos Gingersnap Tea - 58

Main Courses

Antipasti Salad - 106
Baby Back Ribs (Costillitas) - 156
Chicken, Pan-Seared with Onions and Mushrooms - 126
Chicken Nuggets with Honey Mustard - 262
Costillitas (Baby Back Ribs) - 156
Elk Chops, Grilled with Port Wine Reduction - 246
General Tso's Chicken - 34
Ham, Honey Glazed - 76
Lamb Chops with Rhubarb Chutney - 174
Lobster, Spiny with Drawn Butter - 144
Pescados Asado (Grilled Wahoo) - 158
Pizza Margherita - 112
Pork Loin, Apple-Glazed - 190
Pork Sliders - 260
Rib Roast, Standing with Horseradish Sauce - 276
Salmon, Baked with Lemon and Capers - 110
Sliders, Pork and Veggie - 260
Snapper, Stuffed Red - 142
Spaghetti and "Eyeballs" - 208

Teriyaki Country Ribs - 90
Turkey, Stuffed and Rubbed with Duck Fat and Herbs - 230
Veggie Sliders - 260
Venison Roast, Apple Scented - 244
Wahoo, Grilled (Pescados Asado) - 158

Soups and Salads

Balsamic Tomato and Peach Salad - 96
Beef Heart Stew - 206
Butternut Squash Soup Shooters - 290
Cherry Walnut Salad - 186
Creamy Fennel Slaw with Carrots and Apples - 94
Grapefruit Salad - 74
Micro-greens with Diced Mango - 140
No'tato Salad - 92
Poached Pear Salad - 224
Pomegranate Salad, Winter - 272
Pumpkin Chicken Chili - 188
Watermelon Salad with Mint - 124
Wild Mushroom Soup - 242
"Wonton" Soup - 24

Sauces, Dressings and Dips

Avocado Cream - 72
Fig Balsamic Vinaigrette - 186
Hollandaise Sauce - 44
Honey Mustard - 262
Horseradish Sauce - 276
Mango Salsa - 146
Mayonnaise - 92
Olive Tapenade Trio - 60
Pear Guacamole - 204
Port Wine Reduction - 246
Rhubarb Chutney - 174
Sesame Dipping Sauce - 26
Spinach and Artichoke Dip - 258

Side Dishes

Acorn Squash, Baked - 194
Apple Veal Stuffing - 228
Applesauce, Honeycrisp - 192
Arroz Azafrán (Saffron Rice) - 160
Asparagus, Roasted with Bolete Mushrooms - 44
Asparagus, Pan-Fried with Tomatoes - 108
Balsamic Vegetables - 128
Cabbage, Roasted Green and Purple - 278
Carrots, Roasted Rainbow - 80
Cranberry Relish with Dates - 222
Green Beans, Lemon with Shallots - 226
Japanese Eggplant with Onions and Sage - 176
Long Beans with Mushroom Sauce - 32
Marrow Bones, Roasted - 204
No'tato Salad - 92
Potato, Petite Trio - 248
Plantains, Fried with Mango Salsa - 146
Plantain Chips, Fried - 204
Rice, Saffron (Arroz Azafrán) - 160
Shrimp-Fried Rice - 30
Spring Rolls with Sesame Dipping Sauce - 26
Stir-Fried Vegetables - 28
Sweet Potatoes, Candied (See "Yams") - 274
Sweet Potato Hash with Rosemary - 48
Sweet Potato Soufflé - 78
Yams, Candied - 274
Yorkshire Puddings - 280
Yuca con Mojo - 154
Yuca with Garlic Sauce - 154

recipe index

A

Acorn Squash, Baked - 194

Affogato (Coffee) - 116

Aioli, Macadamia Nut - 170

Almond Cookies - 36

Antipasti
    Salad - 106
    Skewers - 296

Apples
    Apple-Glazed Pork Loin - 190
    Apple Pie with a Lattice Crust - 132
    Apple-Scented Venison Roast - 244
    Apple Veal Stuffing - 228
    Caramel "Crab" Apples - 214
    Creamy Fennel Slaw with Carrots - 94
    Honeycrisp Applesauce - 192

Applesauce, Honeycrisp - 192

Arroz Azafrán (Saffron Rice) - 160

Artichokes
    Antipasti Skewers - 296
    Crab-stuffed Artichoke Bottoms - 170
    Green Bean Salad with Artichoke Hearts and Olives - 130
    Spinach and Artichoke Dip - 258

Asparagus
    Bolete-Roasted - 44
    Pan Fried with Tomatoes - 108

Avocado Cream Eggs - 72

B

Baby Back Ribs, Cuban ("Costillitas") - 156

Bacon-Wrapped Shrimp - 124

Baked Acorn Squash - 194

Baked Salmon with Lemon and Capers - 110

Balsamic
    Cherry and Walnut Salad with Fig Balsamic Vinaigrette - 186
    Fig Balsamic Vinaigrette - 186
    Grilled Vegetables - 128
    Tomato and Peach Salad - 96

Beans
    Green Bean Salad with Artichoke Hearts and Olives - 130
    Lemon Green Beans with Shallots - 226
    Long Beans with Mushroom Sauce - 32

Beef
    Beef Heart Stew - 206
    Spaghetti and "Eyeballs" - 208
    Standing Rib Roast - 276

Berries
    Blackberry Cobbler with Vanilla Bean Ice Cream - 178
    "Bleeding" Cupcakes with Raspberry Filling - 210
    Blueberry Lemon Muffins - 98
    Cranberry Relish with Dates - 222

Beverages
    Mimosas - 42
    Rooibos Gingersnap Tea - 58

Birthday Cake, Checkerboard - 264

Birthday Party - 252-264

Biscotti, Chocolate Chip - 114

Biscuits (See "Yorkshire Puddings") - 280
Black and White Bone Cookies - 212
Blackberry Cobbler - 178
Blueberry, Lemon Muffins - 98
Bones, Marrow - 204
Braised Pork Belly - 46
Bread
    Burger Buns - 260
    Crostini - 294
    French - 294
    Yorkshire Puddings - 280
    Zucchini - 64
Burgers
    Buns - 260
    Pork Sliders - 260
    Veggie Sliders - 260
Butter Cream Frosting - 264
Butternut Squash Soup Shooters - 290

C

Cabbage, Roasted Green and Purple - 278
Cakes
    Checkerboard Birthday Cake - 264
    Coffee Cake, Sour Cream - 282
    Pumpkin Torte with Cream Cheese Frosting and Caramel - 196
Candied Yams - 274
Candy Apples - 214
Capers, Baked Salmon with Lemon - 110
Caramel
    Apples - 214
    Pumpkin Torte with Cream Cheese Frosting and Caramel - 196
    Sauce, Coconut Flan - 162

Carrots
    Creamy Fennel Slaw, with Apples - 94
    Carrots with Olive Tapenade Trio - 60
    Rainbow, Roasted - 80
    Veggie Sliders - 260
Cashew, Spinach and Artichoke Dip - 258
Cassava (See "Yuca") - 154
Cauliflower
    Arroz Azafrán (Saffron Cauliflower Rice) - 160
    Shrimp-Fried Rice - 30
Checkerboard Cake - 264
Cheese Pizza (Margherita) - 112
Cherry and Walnut Salad - 186
Chestnuts, Apple Veal Stuffing with - 228
Chicken
    General Tso's - 34
    Nuggets - 262
    Pan-Seared with Onions and Mushrooms - 126
    Pumpkin Chicken Chili - 188
Soup Stock - 290
Chili, Pumpkin Chicken - 188
Chinese Food - 24-36
Chocolate
    Checkerboard Cake - 264
    Chocolate Chip Biscotti - 114
    Dark Chocolate Gelato - 116
    Martinis, Mini - 298
Chops, Lamb with Rhubarb Chutney - 174
Christmas Dinner (See "Winter Holiday Dinner") - 266-282
Cinnamon Maple Hot Cakes - 50
Cobbler, Blackberry - 178
Cocktail Party - 284-298
Cocktail Wieners (Pigs in a Blanket) - 292

Coconut Flan - 162

Coffee Cake, Sour Cream - 282

Cole Slaw, Creamy Fennel with Carrots and Apples - 94

Cookies
  Almond - 36
  Biscotti, Chocolate Chip - 114
  Black and White Bones - 212
  Mummy Cookies - 212
  Scones (See Scones) - 62

Costillitas (Cuban Baby Back Ribs) - 156

Country Ribs, Teriyaki - 90

Crab-stuffed Artichoke Bottoms - 170

Crackers, Herb - 258

Cranberry Relish with Dates - 222

Crème Brûlée - 250

Crème Fraîche
  Avocado Cream Eggs - 72
  Horseradish Sauce - 276

Crescent Dogs (See "Pigs in a Blanket") - 292

Crockpot - 192, 240, 244, 290
  Apple-Scented Venison Roast - 244
  Honeycrisp Applesauce - 192

Crostini - 294

Cuban Dishes - 148-162

Cucumber and Salmon Bites - 60

Cupcakes (See also "Muffins")
  "Bleeding" Cupcakes - 210

Custards
  Crème Brûlée - 250
  Coconut Flan - 162

D

Dates
  Cranberry Relish with Dates - 222
  Pecan Pie - 232
Dips
  Spinach and Artichoke - 258
  Honey Mustard - 262
Duck Fat
  Stuffed Turkey Rubbed with Duck Fat and Herbs - 230

E

Easter - 66-82
Eggplant, Japanese with Onion and Sage - 176
Eggs
  Avocado Cream - 72
  Easter, Dyed - 69
  Eggs Benedict - 44
  Poached (Benedict) - 44
Eggs Benedict - 44
Elk, Grilled Chops with Port Wine Reduction - 246
Espresso Glaze - 282

F

Fennel, Slaw with Carrots and Apples - 94
Figs
  Compote with Goat Cheese - 294
  Fig Balsamic Vinaigrette - 186
Fingerling Potatoes, Petite Potato Trio - 248
Fish
  Baked Salmon with Lemon and Capers - 110

Cucumber and Salmon Bites - 60
Pescados Asado (Grilled Fish) - 158
Stuffed Red Snapper - 142
Flan, Coconut - 162
French Bread - 294
Fried Plantains with Mango Salsa - 146
Frostings
Butter Cream Frosting - 264
Coconut Cream Frosting - 212
Cream Cheese Frosting with Caramel - 196
Dark Chocolate Icing - 210
Espresso Glaze - 282

G

Game Meats
Apple-Scented Venison Roast - 244
Grilled Elk Chops - 246
Sweet and Tangy Venison Meatballs - 240
Garden Party - 118-132
Gelato, Dark Chocolate - 116
General Tso's Chicken - 34
Gorgonzola, Poached Pear Salad with Spiced Pecans - 224
Grape Juice, Poached Pear Salad - 224
Grapefruit Salad - 74
Green Beans
Salad with Artichoke Hearts and Olives - 130
Lemon Green Beans with Shallots - 226
Grilled Balsamic Vegetables - 128
Grilled Elk Chops with Port Wine Reduction - 246
Guacamole, Pear - 204

H

Halloween Recipes - 198-214
Ham, Honey Glazed - 76
Hollandaise Sauce - 44
Heart, Beef Stew - 206
Herb Crackers - 258
Honey
Glazed Ham - 76
Mustard - 262
Horseradish Sauce - 276
Hot Cakes, Cinnamon Maple - 50

I

Ice Cream
Dark Chocolate Gelato - 116
Vanilla Bean - 178
Italian Recipes - 100-116

L

Lamb
Pan-Seared Lamb Chops - 174
Lemons
Baked Salmon with Lemon and Capers - 110
Blueberry Muffins - 98
Green Beans with Shallots - 226
Meyer Lemon Tart - 82
Lobster, Spiny Tails with Drawn Butter - 144
Long Beans with Mushroom Sauce - 32

M

Mangoes
    Fried Plantains with Mango Salsa - 146
    Micro-greens Salad with Diced Mango - 140
Margherita Pizza - 112
Marrow Bones, Roasted - 204
Mayonnaise - 92, 94, 262
Meatballs
    Spaghetti and "Eyeballs" - 208
    Venison, Sweet and Tangy - 240
    "Wonton" Soup - 24
Meyer Lemon Tart - 82
Micro-greens Salad with Diced Mango - 140
Mint, Watermelon Salad - 124
Muffins
    Lemon Blueberry - 98
Mummy Cookies - 212
Mushrooms
    Apple Veal Stuffing - 228
    Bolete, Roasted with Asparagus - 44
    Mushroom Sauce - 32
    Pan-Seared Chicken with Onions and Mushrooms - 126
    Wild Mushroom Soup - 242
Mustard, Honey - 262

N

No'tato Salad - 92
Nuggets, Chicken - 262
Nutritional Yeast - 258
Nuts Spiced with Rosemary and Thyme - 172

O

Olives
    Antipasti Skewers - 296
    Green Bean Salad with Artichoke Hearts and Olives - 130
    Spaghetti and "Eyeballs" - 208
    Tapenade Trio with Carrot Slices - 60
Onions
    Japanese Eggplant with Onions and Sage - 176
    Pan-Seared Chicken with Onions and Mushrooms - 126
Orange Scones and Cranberry Scones - 62
Outdoor Dining
    A Taste of Cuba - 148-162
    Backyard Picnic - 84-98
    Garden Party - 118-132
    Tropical Getaway - 134-146
    Urban Escape - 164-178

P

Pan-Seared Chicken with Onions and Mushrooms - 126
Pancakes - See "Hot Cakes" - 50
Peach Balsamic Salad with Tomato - 96
Pears
    Pear Guacamole - 204
    Poached Pear Salad with Spiced Pecans - 224
Pecans
    Pecan Pie - 232
    Poached Pear Salad with Spiced Pecans - 224
    Spiced Nuts with Rosemary and Thyme - 172
Pescados Asado (Grilled Fish) - 158
Petite Potato Trio - 248

Pies
    Apple with a Lattice Crust - 132
    Crust with Almond Flour - 82, 112, 132, 232
    Pecan Pie - 232
Picnic Recipes - 84-98
Pigs in a Blanket - 292
Pineapple
    Candied Yams - 274
    Sweet and Tangy Venison Meatballs - 240
Pizza Margherita - 112
Plantains
    Fried Chips - 146
    Fried with Mango Salsa - 146
Pomegranate Salad with Fig Balsamic Vinaigrette - 272
Pork
    Apple-Glazed Pork Loin - 190
    Costillitas (Cuban Baby Back Ribs) - 156
    Ham, Honey Glazed - 76
    Pork Belly, Braised - 46
    Sliders - 260
    Teriyaki Country Ribs - 90
Pork Belly, Braised - 46
Port Wine Reduction - 246
Potatoes
    Petite Potato Trio - 248
    "No'tato" Salad - 92
    Sweet (See also "Sweet Potatoes") - 78
Prime Rib (Standing Rib Roast) - 276
Pudding, Chocolate - 280
Puddings, Yorkshire - 280
Pumpkin
    Pumpkin Chicken Chili - 188
    Pumpkin Torte - 196
Purple Cabbage, Roasted with Green Cabbage - 278

R

Rainbow Carrots, Roasted - 80
Red Peppers, Roasted - 296
Red Snapper, Stuffed - 142
Rhubarb Chutney - 174
Ribs
    Country-Style Teriyaki - 90
    Cuban Baby Back Ribs ("Costillitas") - 156
Rice, Saffron (Arroz Azafrán) - 160
Roast Venison - 244
Roast Turkey - 230
Rolls
    Burger Buns - 260
    Yorkshire Puddings - 280
Rooibos Gingersnap Tea - 58

S

Saffron Rice (Arroz Azafrán) - 160
Salmon
    Baked, with Lemon and Capers - 110
    Cucumber and Salmon Bites - 60
Salad
    Antipasti Salad - 106
    Balsamic Tomato and Peach Salad - 96
    Cherry and Walnut Salad - 186
    Grapefruit Salad - 74
    Green Bean Salad with Artichoke Hearts and Olives - 130
    Micro-greens Salad with Diced Mango - 140
    Poached Pear Salad with Spiced Pecans - 224
    Pomegranate Salad - 272
    Watermelon Salad with Mint - 124

Salad Dressings
    Fig Balsamic Vinaigrette - 186
    White Balsamic with Spicy Mustard - 224
Satsuma Orange, Winter Pomegranate Salad - 272
Sauces
    Applesauce, Honeycrisp - 192
    Cranberry Relish with Dates - 222
    Fig Compote - 294
    Honey Mustard - 262
    Horseradish Sauce - 276
    Mayonnaise - 92, 94, 262
    Mushroom - 32
    Port Wine Reduction - 246
    Rhubarb Chutney - 174
    Sweet and Tangy - 240
Scones
    Cranberry - 62
    Orange - 62
Seafood (See also, "Fish")
    Bacon-Wrapped Shrimp - 124
    Crab-Stuffed Artichoke Bottoms - 170
    Pescados Asado (Grilled Fish) - 158
    Shrimp-Fried Rice - 30
    Spiny Lobster Tails with Drawn Butter - 144
    Stuffed Red Snapper - 142
Shrimp
    Bacon-Wrapped - 124
    Fried Rice - 30
Slaw, Creamy Fennel with Carrots and Apple - 94
Slow Cooker (See "Crockpot")
Snapper, Stuffed Red - 142
Soufflé, Sweet Potato - 78
Soups
    Beef Heart Stew - 206

Butternut Squash - 290
Pumpkin Chicken Chili - 188
Wild Mushroom Soup - 242
"Wonton" Soup - 24
Sour Cream Coffee Cake - 282
Spaghetti and "Eyeballs" - 208
Spiced Nuts with Rosemary and Thyme - 172
Spinach and Artichoke Dip - 258
Spiny Lobster Tails with Drawn Butter - 144
Spring Rolls, Steamed with Sesame Dipping Sauce - 26
Squash
    Baked Acorn Squash - 194
    Butternut Squash Soup Shooters - 290
Standing Rib Roast - 276
Stews (See also "Soups")
    Beef Heart Stew - 206
Stir-Fried Vegetables - 28
Stuffed Red Snapper - 142
Stuffed Turkey Rubbed with Duck Fat and Rosemary - 230
Stuffing, Apple Veal - 228
Sweet Potato
    Candied (Yams) - 274
    Hash, with Rosemary - 48
    Petite Potato Trio - 248
    Soufflé - 78
    Yams, Candied - 274
Sweet and Tangy Venison Meatballs - 240
Sweet Potato Hash with Rosemary - 48

T

Takeout - 18-36
Tart, Meyer Lemon - 82

Tea Party - 52-64

Tea, Rooibos Gingersnap - 58

Thanksgiving Recipes - 216-232

Tomatoes

    Balsamic Salad with Peach - 96

    Micro-greens Salad with Diced Mango - 140

    Pan-Fried Asparagus - 108

Torte, Pumpkin - 196

Tostones (Fried Plantains) - 146

Tropical Getaway - 134-146

Turkey

    Stuffed and Rubbed with Duck Fat and Herbs - 230

    Stuffing, Apple Veal - 228

V

Vanilla

    Butter Cream Frosting - 264

    Crème Brûlée - 250

    Ice Cream - 178

Veal, Apple Stuffing - 228

Vegetables

    Balsamic, Grilled - 128

    Sliders - 260

    Stir Fried - 28

Veggie Burgers (Sliders) - 260

Venison

    Apple Scented Venison Roast - 244

    Sweet and Tangy Meatballs - 240

W

Wahoo (Pescados Asado) - 158

Watermelon Salad with Mint - 124

Wild Mushroom Soup - 242

Winter Holiday Dinner - 266-282

"Wonton" Soup – 24

Y

Yams, Candied - 274

Yorkshire Puddings - 280

Yuca con Mojo (Yuca with Garlic Sauce) – 154

Z

Zucchini Bread - 64

...ll Party

t Squash Soup
ooters

n a Blanket

ith Goat Cheese
ig Compote

sti Skewers

olate Martinis

Chicken Nuggets with Honey Mustard

Checkerboard Cake

---

hunter gatherer feast

first
smoked elk loin with wild pear
sweet and tangy venison meatballs
stuffed crimini mushrooms
with fried quail eggs

soup
wild mushroom soup

main
apple scented venison roast
grilled elk chops with port wine reduction

side
petite potato trio
steamed green beans with black truffle salt

dessert
creme brulee with raspberries

HARVEST DINNER

- CHERRY WALNUT SALAD
  WITH FIG BALSAMIC VINAIGRETTE

- PUMPKIN CHICKEN CHILI

- APPLE GLAZED PORK LOIN

- HONEYCRISP APPLESAUCE

- BAKED ACORN SQUASH

- PUMPKIN TORTE WITH CREAM CHEESE
  FROSTING AND CARAMEL

Urban Escape

crab stuffed artichoke bottoms

spiced nuts with rosemary and thyme

pan seared lamb chops
with rhubarb chutney

sauteed japanese eggplant
with onions and sage

blackberry cobbler
with vanilla bean ice cream

Trop... Geta...

micro-greens

stuff...

spiny lobster

fried planta...

...R HOLIDAY

...megranate Salad
...samic Vinaigrette

...died Yams

...g Rib Roast
...seradish Sauce

...d Green and
...e Cabbage

...ire Puddings

...m Coffee Cake

Spooky Supper

Roasted Marrow Bones

**Ghostly Pear Guacamole
with Fried Plantain Chips**

Beef Heart Stew

Spaghetti and "Eyeballs"

"Bleeding" Cupcakes

Mummy Cookies

A TASTE OF CUBA

Mid... Gard...

Waterm...

Bacon...

Pan
with Onio...

Grilled...

Apple Pi...